The Master
of His Game

*To my New Friend
Helana!*

Kenneth E. Roberts

Ken Roberts

ISBN- 978-0692094488

Published by Candy Publishing, LLC
www.candypublishing.net

Printed in the United States of America

Cover Design

DK1 Promotions

Editors

Susie Yale Roberts
Sandra L. Winborne, Ph.D.

DEDICATION

This story would not be possible without Mara Roberts
and Susie Yale Roberts who sacrificed their time to do
many hours of editing on this story.
I thank them and give them full credit for helping me
realize one of my dreams.

When you get to the big city, or maybe even on
this train, you will meet a man who will offer to
bet you ten dollars that he can make a spout
of water shoot up from his head strong enough to
hit the ceiling.

No son, do not bet him. For when it comes to
money, man can do anything.

Advice to Damon Runyon from his father

PREFACE

This book is filled with unbelievable stories - a real look at the life one man lived. A life that most people only dream about.

At twenty-six years of age, Jason Alan Keeble was a man who was obsessed with the reputation of being the smoothest con man since Joseph "Yellow Kid" Weil. He had more material things than the average person will ever see. But deep inside him was a man who loved his wife, loved his children, loved his home and wanted to enjoy a normal life.

Throughout his life, he struggled with real life, his obsession with the road and his only true love. The cons.

THE MASTER
OF HIS GAME

THE GAME

PART I

JASON KEEBLE

1

"My candle burns at both ends,

It will not last the night;

But ah, my foes, and oh, my friends-

It gives a pretty light."

Oscar Wilde

The shiny new Nineteen Fifty-Three Lincoln sedan rolled along the back country road as the evening sun shone brightly on its deep white paint. Jason Keeble sat comfortably in the back seat, enjoying a cool breeze blowing through the window. He was staring at the notes he had made on a piece of paper while Tommy, his driver, cruised along at forty mph snapping his fingers to the rhythm of Benny Goodman on the radio.

Tommy was barely twenty years old, six years Jason's junior and, for the most part, let his zipper do his thinking. Jason had met Tommy through a friend who said Tommy was a real slick kid and all he needed was a little polishing to become a fine con artist. When Jason asked Tommy if he knew anybody who had a fat bankroll and a greedy heart, Tommy jumped to tell him about a man named Johnson he knew in Kentucky who owned a large grocery store and had more money than he could ever spend.

To look at Tommy's face as he sat at the wheel of that big Lincoln, you would guess he was on his way to the big city for the first time, but in reality he was about to be part of a con game that would take about a week to play and net him a full year's salary.

As Jason traveled, he would rehearse his lines for the part he was to play with each new mark. A "mark" is how con artists refer to the person they are about to cheat out of money. This one was going to take some extra effort since he'd just taken Tommy on as a new partner. Tommy would have to play a major part in this one.

As they rode along, Tommy stared at Jason in the rearview mirror and saw the concerned look on his face and thought, "Here I am about to play the cons with a man the old guys say is the smoothest con since Yellow Kid Weil." Just then the thought struck him that it was HE who had told Jason about this guy in Kentucky. Suddenly a cold chill came over him at the thought of them being on some wild goose chase. The truth was that Tommy had simply overheard another con named Harry talking about how he had stopped in Kentucky at this store and how the owner would be easy pickings for a few thousand. Tommy turned the radio down until all that could be heard was the big Lincoln's engine humming. As his nervous eyes looked in the mirror at Jason, he cleared his throat and almost squealed trying to get out the words, "Don't worry Jason, I told you this guy is so full of greed his little heart will explode when he sees the doors fly open on that truck." Jason slowly raised his head from his notes, made eye contact in the mirror with Tommy and replied, "Kid, I'm not worried." A smile came over his face as he went on. "Harry says to tell you thanks to his big mouth, this one is on him."

Jason was a very flamboyant man of twenty-six who would settle for nothing less than the best things in life. He stood six feet tall and one hundred and ninety-five pounds, his dark tanned body looked as though his days were spent at health clubs and on the tennis courts. The truth was that he abused his body all the time but somehow he never showed it.

Just as Tommy spotted the sign that read Lexington Kentucky city limits, Jason said to him, "Pull in there at the White Pillars Hotel, it's close enough to our mark. If you go much farther into the country, we'll have to tote our water in with buckets."

The White Pillars Hotel

The giant white building was nothing like Tommy had ever seen. From the outside, it looked like a castle he'd seen in pictures. Its white pillars stood tall and straight. The doorman stood very properly outside the hotel and his uniform looked like something a general in the army would wear.

As Tommy brought the car to a stop, two young boys suddenly approached the car in what Tommy thought was an attempt to rob them. Then quickly the door sprang open and one of the boys said with a smile, "Welcome gentlemen, to the fabulous White Pillars. Are there bags to be taken in?" Tommy sat there with his mouth wide open while Jason replied, "Thank you, boys, our bags are in the trunk and please put the car in a safe place." He then reached out to the boy with a ten dollar bill in his hand and continued, "I'd be real upset if anything happened to this car." The boy looked at the ten with surprised eyes and replied, "Oh! Sure! And we'll even wash it for you, sir."

As Tommy and Jason walked towards the hotel, it seemed to get larger with each step. Tommy knew it would be a very expensive place to stay. Knowing he had less money than the tip Jason had given to the young boy, Tommy said, "Jason, I'm sure we could find something cheaper if we look around." Jason looked at him with a grin and replied, "Kid, the first thing you have to learn is that I don't do anything cheap and, besides, we might take this guy for a million bucks." Jason laughed aloud.

The doorman opened the big door as they approached and said, "Welcome gentlemen, I hope your stay is a pleasant one." Jason put a couple of dollars in his hand and replied, "I'm sure it will be." As they stepped inside the hotel, all Tommy saw was a vivid red. It looked like a very expensive whorehouse, but he knew better.

They checked into a suite with two bedrooms and a living room. Jason had asked for a suite and, as they walked in, Tommy thought, "Yes, this is a suite. Real sweet."

The rest of the day they just laid around the pool relaxing, or at least Jason was relaxing. Tommy was a bundle of nerves just being there and never failed to trip over his tongue when the waitress came around in her swimsuit. Jason soon met three girls by the pool who were on their way to Florida for a vacation. After two hours of drinking and a little cocaine, Tommy knew the night ahead would be a long one.

That night did seem to last forever, then suddenly the phone rang, jolting Tommy from a deep sleep. "Good morning, this is the front desk. You have a wake-up call for six o'clock a.m. Have a nice day." The phone went dead and as Tommy sat up on the side of his bed he looked over to discover that the girl in his bed was not the same one he had fallen asleep with. As he staggered toward the bathroom he passed Jason's room and couldn't resist peeking in. Jason lay sleeping quietly with the other two girls, one on each side. In the bathroom, Tommy stared at himself in the mirror and thought, "God, I've snorted some cocaine in my life but that shit last night had me high enough to jump all three of those girls. Or maybe I did." He laughed and stepped into the cold shower. Once he was awake he slipped into the old jeans and a pullover shirt he had brought along for his "costume." That was the word Jason used but, to Tommy, those clothes were among the best he had.

After the small breakfast Tommy was able to get down, he phoned a cab and as it drove up, he thought, "Well, it's showtime." He had the cab stop at the first used car lot he saw. The salesman couldn't understand why Tommy wanted the old Nineteen Forty-Eight Chevy coupe. He'd been saving it for a sucker but this kid seemed to know exactly what he wanted. Tommy bought it in a fake name for one hundred dollars, checked the oil and water and drove straight to the Buy-Rite grocery store on Daniel Street. He parked the old car outside the mark's store to make sure it could be easily seen. With his best nervous face, Tommy strolled into the store. There was only one customer in the store so he pretended to look at some canned goods until the lady left. When the owner spotted him, he spoke up, "Can I help you boy?" "Oh yes sir, I need to talk to you." Tommy went almost behind the counter to be sure he got the attention of the owner, whose name was Luther Johnson. "Mister, I have ten cartons of cigarettes that aren't exactly mine and I need to sell them. I know they're worth three dollars a carton, so I'll let them go for one dollar each if you'll take all ten cartons." Johnson looked at him for a minute and replied, "Who the hell are you boy?" Tommy said, "You don't know me sir. I got your name from a traveling salesman who said you were always looking for a bargain. If you're afraid of the cigarettes, I'll try someone else." Tommy knew that was a bold statement but after all, Harry did say the guy was really greedy. As Tommy headed for the door, Johnson said, "Hold on boy, where are the cigarettes?" Tommy sighed with relief and replied, "They're in the car." He brought the cigarettes in and after examining them, Johnson paid Tommy and made him promise to leave town.

Tommy drove back to the hotel where Jason was now sleeping alone. The three girls had gone off to breakfast together. Tommy was so excited about Johnson taking the bait that he stormed into Jason's bedroom yelling, "Get up Jason, the fish took the bait. We've got him." Jason leisurely sat up on the side of the bed, reached for the vile of cocaine, snorted two big lines and with a smile said to Tommy, "Kid, I'm tempted to just call Johnson and tell him to send me two or three thousand to just get in my car and drive away."

They both laughed aloud.

Three days later, Tommy went back and sold Johnson twenty-five more cartons of cigarettes and clued him in about a big deal that might take place soon.

On a third visit to the mark's store, Tommy told him, "Mr. Johnson, the truth of this cigarette thing is that my friend works at the warehouse in Louisville and has access to those cigarettes and now he's offered me a deal on several cases." The mark's eyes lit up on the word "cases." Tommy saw his reaction and knew it would be real easy now and big money wouldn't scare the mark off. Tommy went on, "Mr. Johnson, I can get two hundred cases of cigarettes on a one-time deal. The only thing I need is a truck, so here's what I'll do. You furnish the truck and the two hundred cases of cigarettes are yours for three thousand dollars. You and I both know that's less than half the price they are worth. The two hundred cases will retail for over thirty-six dollars a case." The mark thought it over a bit and greed hit him. "Ok, it's a deal." Tommy smiled to himself and continued, "You'll get a phone call from the guy at the warehouse today because he wants to make sure you aren't someone I've made up. He worries a lot about getting beat out of his big deal. His name is Nicky, and he'll give you all the details." (Nicky was an alias Jason often used when he was on the road.) Johnson didn't like involving other people but Tommy convinced him there would be no problems. Tommy decided to hang around the store and drink a coke to make sure that Johnson didn't have second thoughts. Then he paid for the coke and drove back to the hotel. Johnson let him pay for the coke and that just reconfirmed Tommy's thoughts about Johnson's greed.

That evening Jason, posing as Nicky, phoned the mark, "This is Nicky, do you know a guy named Tommy?" "Yes I do," replied Johnson. "Good," said Jason, "Here's the deal. Tomorrow is Friday; have a twelve-foot box truck at your store at seven-thirty a.m. Tommy will pick it up, then you meet me in the Woolworth parking lot on Salem Road at one-thirty and park under the big sign out front. I will be driving a white Lincoln sedan. Bring the money in cash and bring as many hundred dollar bills as you can so no one notices you with a big bundle of money. Put the money in your own bank bag and be sure you don't try to double-cross us with the police." The mere word police made Johnson's face turn pale white. As he gasped for a short breath, Johnson snapped at Jason, "What about the delivery to my place?" "Don't worry about that," Jason told him. "Tommy will take the truck wherever you tell him to." When they hung up, Jason turned to Tommy in their hotel room and said, "Kid, order us a steak as big as Hank Williams' guitar. Tomorrow we'll both have an ass pocket full of money." They laughed and spent the rest of that day eating and laying by the pool.

On Friday morning, Tommy woke up to a phone call from the front desk. It was six a.m. and he had to be at the mark's store by seven-thirty to pick up the truck. His head was splitting from the whiskey and his hands were shaking from not sleeping. He dressed and slipped out to the restaurant for some breakfast. As he sat there with his coffee, he thought, "If I were that idiot at the store, I'd never fall for such a fool trick, but I guess Jason knows what he's doing or he wouldn't be asleep without a care in the world."

After breakfast, Tommy jumped into the old Chevy and drove to Johnson's store. The truck was there like Johnson promised it would be. When Tommy got inside, Johnson was yelling about his being late. That was a sure sign of nerves. Tommy said, "Mr. Johnson, I'm sorry but my car broke down." When he calmed Johnson down he continued, "If you don't mind I'll have to leave my car here so I was wondering if you could put it around back. That car is all I have and I don't want anyone to steal it." Johnson replied, "I'll take care of the damn car, just get your ass over there and get my cigarettes." Tommy handed him the keys to the old Chevy and left.

When Tommy got back to the hotel room, he was so excited he burst into the room yelling, "Wake up Jason, it's showtime. The truck was there just like you said it would be. It's outside full of gas waiting for your magic touch." Jason showered and crawled into his Levi jeans, a Botany Five Hundred pullover shirt and a pair of handmade alligator boots. Tommy was talking faster than a horse could run but couldn't help noticing what pains Jason took in getting dressed. Jason noticed Tommy watching him and said, "Hey kid, remind me to take you shopping for some new threads when this game is over." "Sure Jason," Tommy replied. But he felt that no clothes could ever make him look as good as Jason.

Once outside, they got a stack of empty cigarette cases from Jason's Lincoln, put them into the truck and drove to a deserted road. As Tommy watched, Jason tied a rope to the inside handle of the rear doors and stretched the rope through the interior of the box truck and continuing on into the truck's cab through a hole he knocked in the back wall of the cab. Next, he sat five empty cases of cigarettes across the tail end of the truck, nailed them down securely to the floor, then poured glue on the top of them and stacked more identical cases on top of them until the entire back of the truck was filled with a wall of cigarette cases. This made the truck look as though it was full of cigarettes. Of course all the cases were empty. Next, Jason took six loose cartons of real cigarettes and, as he closed the doors, he wedged them between the doors and the wall of stacked, empty cases. Finally, Jason pulled the rope tight inside the cab so it would hold the doors closed without having to lock the doors. "That's it, kid." Jason went on, "When the doors swing open, your mark will swear he sees his fortune."

One fifteen came and Tommy got into the box truck to meet the mark. Jason said to Tommy, "Don't worry kid, it'll be a breeze. Just do everything I told you and when you get to the meeting place, act real nervous...and kid, don't fuck this up."

Tommy drove the box truck to an open lot near enough to the meeting place so that he could see when Johnson drove in and there he waited. He wouldn't have to "act" nervous because, deep inside, his guts were in knots. He could just see this fool Johnson jumping out of the car with a pistol and shooting both him and Jason. It would be all his fault. Just about that time, Jason pulled into the Woolworth's parking lot in his Lincoln. Soon the mark also pulled into the lot and came to a stop next to Jason's car. Jason signaled the mark to get in the car with him. Tommy was waiting the five minutes that Jason had told him he needed. It felt like an hour. Once Johnson got into Jason's car, Jason said to the mark, "I don't expect this to take long. Did you bring the money?" The mark replied, "I've got the money. Where are the cigarettes?" Jason said, "They'll be here any minute. Now let me see the money." Johnson handed over a bank bag with a lock on it; a key sticking out of the lock. Jason opened it and flipped through the money, pretending to count it. Then he said, "I don't have time to count this so I'll have to take your word for it that it's all here." Just then, Tommy drove onto the lot, picked up speed and rushed past Jason's car so the mark could see the rear of the truck. Trying to stop, Tommy hit the brakes, let off the pedal and hit them again to jar the truck; then he let go of the rope that had been holding the rear doors shut, so the rear doors swung wide open. The loose cartons of cigarettes flew out, hitting the ground and Jason could see the mark's eyes light up with fear. Then Jason spoke up and said, "What in the fuck is wrong with that fool kid? Don't he know that people are looking right at him?" Now the mark was starting to twist around in his seat, which was exactly what Jason wanted. Then Tommy ran to the back of the truck, picked up the loose cartons and opened the doors one more time so the mark could get a good close look. He then packed the loose cartons of cigarettes back into the truck, closed the doors and this time, locked them. Still acting like some punk kid, Tommy then ran over to Jason's car. Jason rolled the window down and grabbed him by the shirt yanking his head into the car window and yelled, "You fucking idiot, how in the hell did you let those doors fly open like that?" Tommy gasped and replied, "I don't know. I just hit the brakes and they stuck so I let up and hit them again, then I heard something fall." "You punk." Jason continued, "I ought to kick your ass. Get in the car."

Tommy got into the back seat of the car and by this time he and Jason had the mark ready to run at any second. Tommy spoke up and said, "Look, you guys hurry up with this, I don't want anybody to call the police." Jason looked at him and replied in a calm voice, "Just take it easy kid, it's okay." Then, as Jason turned back to talk to the mark, Tommy spoke up and yelled to Johnson, "I'll be at your store with the truck." Without giving the mark time to respond, Tommy hopped out of the Lincoln and ran back to the box truck. Jason yelled at him but Tommy didn't look back. Jason looked over at the mark and said, "That damn fool kid, here's what we'll do." With that, Jason took the money out of the mark's bag and placed it inside a bank bag that was laying on his dash. He locked the bank bag and said, "Just take this bag and give it to the kid when you meet him at the store." Just as the guy reached for the bag Jason pulled it back and said, "If someone is watching us, you don't need to get out with a bank bag." Jason thought a second then continued, "Hand me that paper bag down there by the door panel. We'll put the bag in that and at least you won't look so conspicuous." By this time the mark was so nervous he couldn't think straight if he wanted to. As he reached for the paper bag, Jason secretly switched the real bank bag with one just like it filled with dollar bill sized pieces of newspaper. When the mark turned around, Jason handed him the fake bank bag and instructed him to put it into the paper bag. Jason then said to the mark, "The more I think about it, you and that kid might try to steal my cigarettes. You take the money and go to your store. I'll be right behind you." Johnson agreed and got into his car. As he drove away he thought, "When I get to the store, I will call a friend of mine at the Sheriff's Department and have him come over and scare these punks away and I will end up with the cigarettes and all the money."

Jason then drove up to the front of the shopping center where Tommy stood waiting. Tommy had driven the box truck around to the back of the shopping center and walked through to the front. Jason slid over to let the kid drive and as Tommy got into the car, Jason said, "Calm down kid, it's over. Now drive us out to the main road. I want to go to Atlanta, Georgia." Tommy pulled away from the store and asked, "Did you get the money?" Jason smiled and replied, "Kid, I always get the money." With that, he showed Tommy the bank bag. "Did you count it yet?" Tommy asked. Jason looked at him again and said, "Now, you know that nice man wouldn't try to shortchange us. Besides, the money doesn't matter, it's how well you play the game." Tommy calmed down a little and with a smile asked, "Hey Jason, what do you call that game?" Jason replied, "The bag change. When Johnson finds his truck behind that building and finds it empty he'll look in that bag and realize why I call it that. But there is a good side to it: he does have your nice old Chevy and I'm sure he'll appreciate that." They both laughed. Then Jason continued, "Now let me tell you about this mark I heard about in Orlando, Florida."

I never cheated an honest man, only rascals. They wanted something for nothing. I gave them nothing for something.

Joseph "Yellow Kid" Weil

2

Frank and Christine

Christine Keeble picked up the phone and scrambled through her address book until she found the number to a roadhouse across town. She asked for her husband Frank. She knew he would be there because it was his regular Wednesday night poker game. He was also trying to stay close to home these days. When Frank answered, Christine said, "Frank, it's time. I feel the baby coming and I don't think he wants to wait much longer. Please meet me at the hospital." There was an attempt to be calm in her voice but Frank could tell that she was in great pain. Frank said to her, "Don't worry honey, I'll be home in a few minutes and everything will be fine." "No." she answered. "The ambulance is already outside. Just meet me in the emergency room."

Frank hung up the phone and told the guys at the poker table, "I've got to leave you fellows. That was my wife. She says Frank Jr. is on the way. I'll catch you next week." Frank Jr. couldn't have picked a better time. A big gambler had shown up that night from Chicago. His purpose for being there was to play poker with the "best poker player in the South," Frank Keeble. Frank figured out right away that he could not outplay this guy but his luck had been good lately, so he figured, what the hell. The gambler started off by letting Frank win several hands totaling about two thousand dollars. Frank was playing his best but he knew a setup when he saw it. As soon as he lost back down to about one thousand dollars, he would simply fall out with a fake heart attack and let the ambulance carry him and the card shark's money away. The call from Christine was indeed right on time.

At eleven thirty-six that night, a son was born to Frank and Christine. When Frank saw him, he could hardly believe that little bundle was his. As he stared at his son he thought, "Dear God, it could only be you who brought us this child. I thank you for him and ask that you bless him well." The boy's skin was a beautiful dark complexion. His hair was a soft blonde which he inherited from his mother. He had many of her features and his body was as sturdy as that of a weight lifter. His arms and legs looked strong and the boy reminded Frank of the gladiators he'd read about when he was a small boy.

Frank and Christine had agreed, if it was a girl, Christine would pick the name but if it was a boy, the choice would be Frank's. Frank wanted to call him "LUCKY" but that would be a hard name for the boy to live with. When Christine woke up from the delivery and Frank told her the name he had chosen, she was very pleased. The birth certificate read, "On August eighth, Nineteen Hundred and Twenty-Eight, at eleven thirty-six p.m. a boy child, Jason Alan Keeble was born to Frank and Christine

Keeble." Frank paid the hospital bill with the big gambler's money and in a few days, drove his wife and son home.

Frank was a self-taught hustler. He knew a few old con games but he mostly made his living with the poker cards, betting on ball games and horse races. He traveled most of the time to gamble in the big games and made enough money to support his family and a handsome three bedroom home in Newnan, Georgia. Newnan was about thirty miles south of Atlanta. Frank had won the house several years back in a card game. Christine fell in love with it, so they decided to call it home.

As Jason grew, Frank was gone a lot of the time. Christine could see that it hurt him to leave the boy but she knew the road pulled at him like a bad habit. When Frank was home, he took the boy everywhere he went so he could show him off. Jason was a fine looking little man at two years old. Frank would even take Jason to a poker game (he didn't mention that part to Christine). By the time Jason was nine years old, he knew well that his father was a favorite with all the girls. Once he caught his father kissing one of the girls at a roadhouse. As they drove home later, Frank was thinking of excuses to tell Christine once the boy told of his day's adventures. Suddenly as though Jason read Frank's mind, he broke the silence saying, "Daddy, you don't have to worry about me telling mother, on you and that lady. We'll just keep what we do on the road between us."

Four months before Jason's fourteenth birthday, his father told him, "Son, I know you've got your eye on a bicycle in the hardware store uptown. Your mother tells me that the man at the grocery store says he can use you as a stock boy for a while. I think it's time you learn the value of working for your money." All the time Frank was thinking to himself, "Who in the hell am I to tell that boy a thing like that?" But it was what Christine wanted. "Son," Frank told him, "Your mother says she has already picked out something else nice for your birthday and that if you want the bicycle, you'll have to earn it." Jason did want the bicycle more than anything else in the world, so he decided to accept the job at the grocery.

After one week at work, Jason missed the time he spent with his father and his friends. He quit the job cold one day just before lunch. He told his mother that he had decided he didn't want the bicycle as much as he thought he did and he just wanted to forget the job and concentrate more on school. His mother was very upset and accused his father of leading the boy astray.

Two days before Jason's birthday he told his father that he needed ten dollars to buy some materials for a science project for school. He had spent the money he earned from the time he had worked at the grocery store but promised his dad that he would pay the ten dollars back by doing odd jobs. Frank decided to let him have the money but didn't mention it to Christine. If the boy paid the money back it would teach him how important money is. Little did Frank know, Jason had already learned the value of money.

Young Lenny Patillo

The next day Jason went to his friend Lenny's house. Lenny always scored A's in penmanship and that would be most helpful in Jason's plan. "Lenny, I need your help." "Sure Jason, just name it." Jason went on, "I want you to take this ten dollar bill and write on it with red ink, 'Happy Birthday Jason.'

I want to make it look like a gift from my father."

On Jason's birthday, Lenny took the ten dollar bill and wrote on it in red ink exactly as Jason had instructed. He put it in his pocket and went to the hardware store uptown. He went to the red bicycle that Jason wanted and looked it over real good. Then he made sure he got the attention of the old man who owned the store just like Jason said to do. "Sir, today is my birthday. My father is buying me a bicycle and this is the one I want." The store owner scratched some figures on a pad he kept in his pocket and said to Lenny, "Sonny, that bicycle is eight dollars and forty-nine cents. Are you sure you can afford that?" Without speaking, Lenny produced the ten dollar bill from his pocket. The old man showed much surprise on his face. He swiftly grabbed the ten and put it in the cash register, noticing the red writing on the bill. Then he counted out the change to Lenny and slammed the drawer of the cash register shut. Lenny hopped on the bicycle and rode it through the store towards the front door while the store owner ran after him yelling not to run over something. Once outside and back in the alley where Jason was waiting, Lenny said, "It went just like you said it would Jase." Jason sighed with relief and replied, "I knew it would work. All we have to do now is wait until the store owner goes to lunch. I've watched him for three days and it looks like he'll go at eleven sharp."

They rode the bicycle and played until ten forty-five, then went back to the alley near the store to wait for the store owner to leave. He left right on time. Jason said to Lenny, "Here goes and remember, if I don't come out in fifteen minutes, just take the bike to your house and hide it in the basement and wait for me." Jason walked calmly into the store and looked around at some things until he saw a lady at the register, then he picked up a new baseball that cost seventy-five cents. He walked to the counter and gave the lady a one dollar bill he got from his allowance. When the lady handed him the twenty-two cents in change, he looked straight at her and said, "Excuse me, ma'am, I gave you a ten dollar bill. Please give me the rest of my change." The lady replied, "Son, you must be mistaken. It was a one dollar bill that you gave me." Jason snapped right back at her. "No ma'am, my daddy gave me ten dollars for my birthday and I can prove it." "How?" the lady asked. "Okay." Jason told her, "My daddy wrote my name on the bill in red. The writing on it says, 'Happy Birthday Jason'. Now, please give me my money or I'll have to call my daddy to come up here and he'll be plenty mad."

The lady looked in the cash register ignoring Jason. There was a ten just like he said, but she was sure in her mind that he had not given her a ten. By this time Jason had made such a fuss that the other store clerk, a younger man, came up to the front. When the lady explained the story to the other clerk, he looked over to Jason and said, "Son, I'm not doubting your word on this but I might have to call your father to verify this since it's such a large difference." Jason felt the show might be over. The store owner would surely be back soon and if this guy called Jason's father all would be lost. Including his ass. Jason thought for a minute as he looked straight at the store clerk and said, "My daddy's at work so you'll have to call him at this number." He produced the number but it wasn't a number at his father's job. It was the roadhouse where his father was gambling. He continued, "You'll be sorry you made him drive up here." The store clerk dialed the number and when he hung up he said to Jason, "Your dad says he did give you a ten dollar bill and he'll be right up here to straighten all this out." Jason's heart fell to his feet. He knew his daddy would kill him. Jason thought to himself, "I'll be in big trouble. Maybe I could tell Daddy that I was just helping Lenny out so I didn't know what was going on. No, that will never work. Daddy is much too sharp to go for that and, besides, I could never bring Lenny into this. I'll just have to take my medicine."

When Frank arrived, he sensed something wasn't right, so he went into the store with a concerned look on his face and said to Jason, "Hello son, what's the problem here?" Jason looked straight at his father but couldn't say a word. The store clerk spoke up and told Frank the entire story except for the part about the writing on the bill in red ink. He wanted to test Frank. "Mr. Keeble, did you write on the ten dollar bill you gave your son?" Suddenly Frank realized what was happening. His mind raced. He recognized that his son was playing an old con—the 'happy birthday trick'. Frank then replied, "Yes I did. Why?" Jason couldn't believe what his father was saying. The store clerk then asked, "And what did you write on the bill?" Frank knew what was supposed to be on the bill because he'd seen the trick done many times but he wasn't sure what his son had put on the bill. Feeling he had no other choice, he took a chance and replied, "I wrote the words 'Happy Birthday Jason' on it in red ink. Why all these questions?" The store clerk's face fell as he handed the bill to Frank and, to Frank's surprise, there was the writing on the bill just as he had described it. The store clerk then asked, "Is that your writing?" Frank looked at the bill again and replied, "Yes that's it." The store clerk then reached into the cash register and pulled out nine dollars which he handed to Jason to make the additional correct change for the ten dollar bill. Frank pretended as if this was all a great inconvenience to him and was apologized to by the embarrassed store clerk.

Once in the car, Jason couldn't speak. Jason's mind raced. "This all took too long," he thought to himself. "What happened to the old man who owns the store? If he had come back from lunch everything would have been ruined." What Jason didn't know was that the store owner had been delayed because he had stopped to collect an overdue account of two dollars on his way back from lunch.

As Frank drove toward the roadhouse, he thought for a while about how to handle this. He was stunned but not angry. Then he said, "Son, that old trick is older than I am, where did you learn about it?" Jason still couldn't hold his head up but finally said, "I heard Cecil telling the girls at the roadhouse how he started out on that game." His father told him, "At your age, it takes heart to try that. I want you to tell me why you did that?" Jason replied, "Daddy, I wanted the bicycle at the hardware store." Frank interrupted, "What bicycle?" Jason replied, "You know, that one I wanted for my birthday. I borrowed the ten dollar bill from you and had my friend write on it. Then my friend took it over to the store and bought the bike with it." "I see, and just who is this friend?" Frank asked with amusement. Jason looked out the window and said in a low voice, "Daddy, you taught me never to tell on people. Do I have to tell you?" Frank silently contemplated the truth in what his son was saying. "Ok son, I'll go along with that. So, you bought the baseball with a one dollar bill but told the lady you gave her a ten, right?" "Yes Daddy," Jason replied. "Well son," Frank continued, "you know it was wrong for you to do that. Your mother would kill both of us if she knew. We'd better try and figure out a way for you to come up with a bicycle without having any money." Jason was in shock that his father was actually going to let him keep the bicycle. As they neared the roadhouse Jason spoke up, "I still owe you ten dollars." With that, he produced the change from the ten he got from the man at the store and added change of his own to make an even ten. Frank watched him count out the money and thought to himself, "My son, a hustler. But at least he pays his debts." When they reached the roadhouse, Frank told Jason, "Call your friend who has the bicycle and tell him to ride it over to Main Street. I'll have one of the boys meet him and bring it to the house tonight where you and I will act very surprised." Jason called Lenny and the bicycle wasn't mentioned anymore that afternoon.

That night after a wonderful birthday dinner that Christine had spent all day preparing, she gave Jason her present, an expensive pair of handmade shoes. He looked at the shoes and thought, "These shoes must have cost a thousand dollars." They shined like glass and were like no other shoes he'd ever seen. His present from Frank was a gold bracelet. It had the name JASON engraved on the inside of it and sparkled beautifully in the light. At that moment Jason Keeble felt a change take place in his life: he was no longer a kid but a grown man. From that day on, only the best would be good enough for him.

When the doorbell rang, Christine said, "Now who could that be at this hour?" As she answered the door, she called to Frank, "It's Cecil." Cecil was Frank's best friend and had been his road partner for many years. Cecil was also an old gambler but he was, above all, an expert at the con games. Jason loved and admired him. When Cecil entered the room he was pushing a bright red bicycle. He pushed it near Jason and said to him, "This is a little birthday present for you from me." Jason grabbed the bicycle and just as his father had told him, he acted as though getting that bicycle was the last thing he ever expected. His mother watched him with the bike and thought, "He really shouldn't get that bike since he wasn't willing to work for it, and I know his father, he had something to do with all this." Jason did look very happy to have the bike, so when he looked to his mother for approval, she hopped on the bike and started riding it around the house. That was approval enough for everyone. As they all watched Christine, Jason was thinking, "I don't even want that bicycle anymore. I'll give it to Lenny in a few weeks. Bicycles are for kids."

Nay, if it be thy will I shall endure,

And sell ambition at the common mart,

And let dull failure be my vestiture,

And sorrow dig its grave within my heart.

Oscar Wilde

3

The world was at war when Frank Keeble's wife became pregnant for the second time. The draft had turned Frank down. His army rejection slip read, "UNDESIRABLE CHARACTER." Jason was fifteen years old now and about to step into manhood. Christine was in her seventh month of pregnancy and anxiously awaiting her new baby. Frank was in New Orleans where he'd been gambling for the past two weeks. When the phone rang at the front desk it was for him. Jason's voice came on the phone, "Daddy, mother is in labor and looks real bad. What should I do?" His father replied, "Son you will have to handle this yourself. Rush her to the hospital and I'll leave for home tonight." Frank spoke to Christine to comfort her and in the middle of his sentence she interrupted and said, "Frank Keeble, I love you with all my heart." Frank hesitated a moment and softly replied, "And I love you, Christine." They hung up the phone with Frank telling her that everything would be fine. While Jason was driving his mother to the hospital, she hemorrhaged. She and the baby both died shortly after they reached the hospital.

When the doctor walked down the hall toward the waiting room Jason read his face and knew his mother was dead. As the doctor started to speak, Jason ignored him and walked straight to her room. He asked the nurses to leave them alone. The baby had been taken away and Christine was covered except for her head. She looked very peaceful to Jason and he talked to her as though she was still alive. He said a silent prayer that she would be with God. Then he kissed her soft face and the stillness of her skin made tears run down his cheeks. He said goodbye to her and walked outside. He wanted his father.

Frank had driven four hours toward home convincing himself that all was going to be alright. However, something didn't feel right inside. A gut feeling told him to call home. When Jason answered the phone, he said, "Daddy, they're both dead." Tears came to Jason's eyes as he waited for his father's reply but Frank remained silent. Minutes passed and Jason said, "Daddy, are you there?" His father was slow to answer, "Yes son. I don't understand it. She was just having a baby." The thing that kept racing through Frank's mind was what Christine had said to him on the phone. It was her goodbye and he hadn't heard what she was saying. He told Jason, "Son, I'll be home soon." They hung up the phone and Frank immediately phoned Cecil. That's when he broke down. "I can't face this right now. Please take care of Jason until I get home. I need some time to deal with this." Frank dropped the phone and walked across the street to a little bar and grill. For the next three days, he wandered from bar to bar, trying to drink it all away.

Christine and the baby were brought to Frank's house. Her family wanted them buried the next day but Cecil stepped in and stopped that. He said, "Frank will be home soon and no one but he and Jason will put them in the ground. He'll be here."

Two days passed while everyone sat waiting for Frank. They barely broke the silence. Cecil could see that Jason was in a daze. "Frank should be here with him." He thought. On the third day, Frank's car pulled into their yard. Everyone was relieved to have him home, but it wasn't home to Frank anymore. Frank ambled to the caskets where he sat recalling his and Christine's life together. After a last goodbye, he closed the caskets.

That next day at eleven o'clock, he and Jason, along with the family, put Christine and the baby to rest. It was that day Jason began to see the meaning of real love. He watched his father and saw the life drain from his face.

Frank bought beautiful headstones for Christine and the baby. When he was asked what he wanted on Christine's stone, Frank thought about the day they met. He had gone to the family reunion of a friend and Christine was there. He spent most of the day charming her, finally leading her to the top of a large hill where he kissed her.

Remembering that day and one of Christine's favorite songs, the stone read:

Christine

"Once on a high and windy hill,
In the morning mist
Two lovers kissed
And the earth stood still."

Paul Frances Webster
"Love is a Many Splendored Thing"

The baby was buried next to Christine and his stone read:

"I am in my mother's arms"

Three weeks passed with Frank ignoring life. He was consumed by memories and guilt. Jason stayed with him faithfully, mainly making sure his father ate. Cecil came by every day to check on them and help Jason with paying the household bills. Jason did all the shopping and learned how to keep the house going. He often thought about how much work his mother had to do, keeping the household together. It made him miss her even more. Time dragged by. There was very little conversation between Frank and his son. Finally, Jason couldn't stand it anymore. He sat down next to his father and told him, "Daddy, I'll never know how this has hurt you but I know mother wouldn't want you to lay down and die. I need you now." It almost seemed his father was ignoring him, however, he continued, "The guys in New Orleans called three times this week. They want you to come down and play poker." Frank lifted his eyes and replied, "Son, if it weren't for you I'd completely give up. This thing has done something to me that I can't explain to you. You're right about one thing, Christine would tell me to get out of this house and make us some money." He smiled a little smile as he thought about her, then he went on, "But son I just can't seem to get over this." Jason spoke up, "Daddy, I know you're gone a lot when you work and you'll have to decide who to leave me with, but before you do, I want to tell you how I feel and what I want." "Okay son," Frank replied. This was their first real talk in a long time. "Daddy, I don't like school. I never have. I went because mother insisted. My place is with you, so I want to quit school and travel with you. I'll stay out of your way and do all I can to earn my keep. Besides, somebody will have to take care of you and make sure you eat right." Just two days ago, Frank had tried to figure out how he'd be able to raise his son with the lifestyle he had and now he was listening to his son solve it with one statement. But dropping out of school was something Christine would never hear of. The boy seemed to be born lucky and though Frank didn't want him to grow up without an education, he was willing to try it Jason's way, providing Jason promised to take some correspondence classes as they traveled.

The next week Frank sold the house and all that was in it, except for their personal things which he carried to Cecil's house. After spending the night with Cecil and his wife Lynn, Frank and Jason left for New Orleans. As they drove, Frank could see that Jason was happy to be on the road. He said a silent prayer to Christine asking her to forgive him. "It's all I know and I swear I'll try to do right by the boy."

Frank went straight to the roadhouse and after some small talk, everyone was introduced to Jason. Soon all the guys went into a little room that looked to Jason as though rats might attack at any time. The card room was smoke-filled, dimly lit and cold. They all sat on wooden chairs and Jason thought, "This is not for me, but I have to start somewhere." Jason could see how the gambling excited his father. Hopefully, it would take his mind off Christine.

Jason learned the basics of gambling, and his father assured him that in a year or so he would be very good with the cards. The second night Jason could stand the boredom of poker cards no longer, so he folded his hand and drifted into the back of the building behind the bar. He found himself in a large room that was beautifully decorated in red and white and looked very classy. He thought to himself, "This is more like it." He soon found out he was in a house of ill repute. This didn't mean much to him at the time. It was during wartime and there weren't many men around. Girls jumped at everything in pants. Jason, only fifteen, walked into the place and girls stormed him as though he was Clark Gable. He didn't know where he was, but he knew that he was going to enjoy this. An older lady soon appeared and took Jason aside. She could see that he liked the girls but she also knew he didn't realize where he was. After finding out he was Frank Keeble's son, she took the boy to her bedroom and that night he lost his virginity.

Jason and Frank found a small apartment near the roadhouse. Jason kept the apartment clean while Frank gambled to make money. Jason soon became the Madame's favorite. She taught him a few tricks and answered a lot of his questions about life and sex. She was the only person Jason had to talk to these days. He worked for the Madame cleaning rooms to earn extra money. Frank had started drinking heavily and losing big at the poker table. The Madame told Jason, "Son, your father loved your mother very much. He talked about her and you all the time. He's not the same since her death. I don't know if he'll ever snap out of this. I'm going to help you make some money because I think you're going to have to start earning the money in your house." The next night the Madame took Jason to her home where wealthy ladies would pay ten dollars to sleep with Jason. The wise old Madame got half of what Jason made and with her personal training, business was very good.

Jason loved his father very much and was trying to support the both of them. Then Frank started taking the money Jason made so he could drink more. He didn't know how Jason earned the money and he didn't care. Jason finally told him, "I do all I can to help support us but you have to stop drinking away the money I earn." Frank blamed the war and the economy for his shortcomings. He said New Orleans just wasn't his town anymore and decided it was time to move on. With about fifty dollars that Jason had saved and a few dollars that Frank's friends let him win, they hit the road again, heading towards Texas. Jason picked up odd jobs in bars and learned all he could about gambling from his father but still had no interest in it. He soon dropped all his correspondence courses in order to work more hours. He knew that he must gather all the street knowledge he could to be able to make it in this world. Jason liked going to the horse track with his father and won sometimes, but like the poker games, the horses were just not a sure enough thing for him.

Jason had a sharp eye for spotting people with big money at the bars. He would steer them from the bars to his house to play poker with his father and two other men, who pretended to be drunk and throwing money around. They would flash the money to make the unsuspecting mark greedy and then drain the guy. Soon it was obvious to the other men that Frank was no longer pretending to be drinking. He was so drunk at the games he could hardly deal the cards. For a while, the other two men were still able to take the suckers for their money, pay Jason for the use of the house, and still make a profit. Finally they got sick of Frank and his drunk crying stories about his deceased wife. They eventually called the games off.

When Frank sobered up and asked about the next game, Jason told him, "Daddy, I miss mother just like you do, but life can't stop just because of her death. Let her rest and let's make some of this easy money that's out there. I'll get the guys back to the poker game if you'll promise to stay sober." Frank agreed although he knew he couldn't live up to his promise to Jason.

That evening Frank robbed a local grocery store for whiskey money. The police caught him and within fifteen days he was sentenced to serve ten years in the Texas Department of Corrections, Huntsville, Texas. Now Jason was suddenly alone and scared.

Texas Department of Corrections

Jason ducked the welfare people in fear they would put him in a foster home. He sold his father's car and when that money was gone he went to the horse track and ran errands for change so he could eat. He slept with the bums near the horse tracks. One day while at the track he spotted an older man that he had noticed placing big bets. The guy had a brace on his back that made it hard for him to get to the window in time to place his bets. Jason sat near him and soon said to the man, "Sir, I'll be glad to make your bets if you'll buy my lunch, but you'll have to tell me what to say when I get to the window." The guy could see the window from his seat so he figured it would be safe to trust the boy. The man never failed to watch Jason to be sure he went to the right window.

After a couple of days, Jason had the old man calling him son, and was invited to dinner at his house after the track closed. Over time Jason noticed the old man could not seem to pick a winner, so Jason started going to the window and pretending to place the bets by betting only a portion of the money. At the end of a day, he could usually stick back about twenty dollars. Now, this was Jason's idea of gambling and as long as the old man continued to lose, it would be a fine place for him to hang out. Then one day the old man got a tip from the track owner who had decided to let him win out of courtesy since he spent so much money there. The bet was two hundred dollars at four-to-one odds. Jason had only placed twenty of the two hundred dollars on the bet so when the horse came in to pay winnings of eight hundred dollars, Jason found the nearest exit and left in a hurry, never to return.

Prison itself is a tremendous education in the need for patience and perseverance. It is above all a test of one's commitment.

Nelson Mandela

"Life is a gamble, at terrible odds – if it was a bet you wouldn't take it

Tom Stoppard

4

Jason was sixteen now and had nowhere to go. He thought of Cecil and how Cecil had helped him and Frank so many times. Cecil spent a lot of time at the roadhouse in New Orleans where Jason had enjoyed his life so much. Jason decided to hitch a ride back to New Orleans where he was welcomed with open arms by the old Madame. She had heard about Frank going to prison through Cecil and they were both worried about where Jason might be.

The girls who worked for the Madame rushed Jason upstairs, gave him a long hot bath, fed him and put him to bed. He'd only been sixteen for a few weeks but he considered himself a grown man. As time passed, Jason grew very fond of one of the girls at the Madame's house and they started spending a lot of time together.

Jason at 16

Her name was Heidi. She had no family and although she really didn't choose to be a working girl, she too had no place else to go. Heidi loved to sleep with Jason and often wore him out long before her own desires were satisfied. Jason went to Heidi's room one night and found her almost drunk on wine. She attacked him, but this particular night was different. She refused to let him burn out. She pulled a small vial from her purse and from it she poured a white powder on the table. She showed Jason how to snort it up his nose and to his surprise, it kept him sexually aroused all night. From then on the powder would become a huge part of his life. The powder was cocaine.

Jason was a big help around the Madame's house, especially when some john would get rough with one of the girls and had to be thrown out. He loved sleeping with some of the girls and hanging out at the house, but he and the Madame both knew that this was not the place for him. The Madame soon got in touch with Cecil who came to pick Jason up. After a long talk with Jason they agreed he would live with him and his wife, Lynn. Cecil had been living in Newnan, Georgia even before Frank and Christine did, so it would again be home for Jason. On the way home, Jason mentioned to Cecil how he worried about his father in prison and would like to visit him sometime. Cecil promised him they'd both visit Frank soon. That made Jason feel somewhat better about all the mess his life was in.

Cecil soon found out that Jason was very different from Frank. Frank loved gambling while Jason studied the con games. He was in a hurry to grow up and be on his own. He told Cecil, "I want to travel with you and learn the big games, I hate hustling for pennies." Cecil's wife wanted to take the boy and raise him properly as Christine would have, but Cecil knew that would be impossible. Jason had already tasted the life he wanted. "Son," Cecil said, "Lynn and I want to raise you the way your mother would, so you stay around the house for a while and see how things go. Then you and I will talk about you traveling with me."

Cecil knew Jason would need money because he had already developed a need to play with the girls, so before he left that next day he bought Jason a car. It was a shiny black 1940 Ford Coupe. Jason loved the car. It was only four years old and looked like new. Jason agreed to earn money to pay Cecil back for the car. As they drove the car home, Cecil said, "Pull in at that hamburger joint and when we go in, listen and watch me closely," They stopped and Cecil approached the lady at the counter saying, "We'd like two large cokes and two orders of fries please."

When the order was ready, Cecil was talking to Jason and without looking up, he placed a ten dollar bill on the counter. When the change came, it was thirty cents in silver, one five dollar bill and four ones. Cecil took the thirty cents and shoved it into his pocket ignoring the other bills. When the girl pushed the bills toward him, he asked her, "Is this mine?" The girl replied, "Yes, you gave me a ten dollar bill." She had already put the ten dollar bill into the cash register. She pulled it back out to show it to him. She then further explained to Cecil, "Your change is the thirty cents I gave you, making one dollar. Four ones make five and five makes ten dollars." Cecil looked real confused and said, "I sure thought I gave you a one dollar bill." Still looking very confused, Cecil fingered through a roll of money he had in his pocket and said, "You're right, I did have a ten in my pocket. He looked at Jason and said, I need to pay closer attention to my money and stop talking." He then looked back at the cashier and said, "I really don't need all these ones, do you have a five for five ones?" She looked in the cash register and replied, "Yes I do." With that, she took a five from the register and handed it to Cecil.

As she reached out with the five, he placed four ones into her hand folded so she wouldn't notice that he had only handed her four ones. He took the five she gave him and went straight to his pocket with it. Then he turned as if to walk away. The cashier said, "Excuse me, sir, you only gave me four ones." Cecil stared at the four ones she had laid out on the counter, then asked, "Are you sure? I could have sworn there were five ones there." The girl replied. "No sir, it was only four." Cecil thought for a minute then said, "Well, if that's four, let's do it this way." He pulled out the rest of his money roll. Then he put a five and a one on the counter and said to the girl, "Here, count this and see if that's ten dollars." As she looked at the bills, Cecil started to count the money out loud and separate it so she could count along with him. "Five, six, seven, eight, nine, ten. Now, is that ten dollars?" "Yes," was her reply. She had become so confused that she forgot the four ones were hers. Then Cecil continued, "Well, suppose you just give me my original ten dollar bill back. I never meant to give it to you anyway." She gave him the ten, he thanked her and then he and Jason left.

Once in the car, Jason said, "Wow, Cecil, you took that girl for four dollars, some change, and this food. I like that trick." Cecil listened to the boy and knew he was a natural at the cons so he gave him fifty dollars in cash to work with and told him, "Jason, you play this little game in the small towns nearby while I'm gone and be sure to stay out of fights in the bars and when you're in heat, leave my wife alone. There's a whorehouse on Fifth Street."

 For the next year, Jason hung out with some old friends of his and played his little ten dollar flim-flam game in all the small towns he could get to without being gone overnight. He never worked at a public job and all his friends resented it very much. He saved some money and bought a better car to impress the few girls he dated. Most of the time he was out of town too much to make dates and he hated holding hands at the movies anyway. Jason preferred real action so he'd just drop by the whorehouse when the urge hit him for sex. He'd found a local connection for his cocaine but only used it when he was with the girls.

 Cecil's wife Lynn loved Jason and enjoyed his company since Cecil wasn't able to be home much. He was a great help around the house and he always had the best manners when he was there. Jason learned a very valuable lesson that year about the true meaning of a real friendship.

One night Lynn came into his bedroom to say goodnight and the next thing he knew, she was in his bed. Lynn was thirty-nine and a beautiful woman. Jason wanted her at that moment more than anything, but then he remembered what Cecil had told him, "Play this little flim-flam game and leave my wife alone." Cecil must have known Lynn needed a man more than he could ever be there for her.

Lynn and Cecil

Jason's passion grew as Lynn slid closer to his body but he felt uneasy – as though he was stabbing Cecil in the back so he stopped her. "Lynn, he told her, "you are a very beautiful lady and I want you more than you could ever know but we just can't do this to Cecil. He's been my friend and it's just not right." Lynn left his room and never tried to sleep with him again. He didn't tell Cecil, and from that day on, Jason vowed he would never sleep with a friend's wife or girlfriend.

At seventeen, Jason was now reconnected with his old friend, Lenny, who he had grown up with. Lenny was still going to school and not very active in any school groups and Jason liked that. He didn't want anybody else to hang around with them. Jason hadn't seen Lenny in a long time but Lenny could be trusted and with a little polish, he would be able to help with the con games that Jason was doing. They seemed to know each other's every move and within two months, were inseparable. Jason taught Lenny the ten dollar flim-flam and showed him the many pleasures of women and cocaine. Lenny's parents didn't care for Jason at all, so Lenny did some slipping around to hang out with him. They traveled together to cities near Newnan and on to Florida one weekend. Jason was itching to take on the open road and much bigger cons. He hoped Cecil would take him out on a big con soon.

Cecil saw that Jason was trying to fly much too fast so he decided to get him out of town for a break. "Why don't we take a little trip to see your dad?" Jason was ready to go and very excited. They drove to the prison in Texas that next day and had a lot of time to talk and bond. Frank was so excited to see Jason that he cried. Jason was relieved that his father wasn't drinking but the prison was working him much too hard. The weekend passed quickly. On Monday, Jason and Cecil left for home with a promise to Frank that they would write and visit when possible. On the way home, Cecil let Jason play his little flim-flam game some to get his mind off seeing his father so worn down.

The next weekend Jason and Lenny pulled into the local hamburger joint. They parked beside a red Mercury. Then something happened to Jason that he'd never slowed down enough to think about. He fell in love. The girl sitting in the red Mercury had long dark hair which fell in soft curls around the most innocent and beautiful face Jason had ever seen. When their eyes met, it was like they both felt something very special happen. They were introduced by a friend of Jason's. Her name was Anna and she was eighteen. Jason couldn't stop staring at her and when he got up the nerve to ask her out, he didn't even get the question out before she yelled, "yes." That weekend they went to the drive-in theatre and just held hands but Jason really enjoyed holding hands with her. It didn't bore him for a minute.

Jason and Anna

Anna's parents were divorced so she lived with her sister and brother-in-law out in the country. She was still in school so Jason started picking her up after school, whenever he was in town. Anna's sister and brother-in-law worked in a factory in town and were gone from three p.m. until midnight. Jason soon began to spend his every night at Anna's house, just the two of them. They were crazy about each other and each day their passion grew. The petting grew heavier each minute they were together. Then one evening they were watching TV and kissing. She let Jason's hand glide up her leg until her stocking stopped and she felt his hand as it paused on her soft inner thigh. She struggled with her desires as Jason explored her beautiful body and when she could stand no more, she asked him to make love to her. Anna was still a virgin, but her overwhelming desire for Jason made everything feel right. Jason drove home that night wondering which was stronger, making love to her, or how he felt in his heart for her. Could this be what love feels like?

They were crazy about each other now, so much that Jason had completely stopped going out of town with Lenny to make money. He was in love and nothing else mattered.

He had a little money stuck back and that should last a lifetime. Or so he thought.

The next year Jason turned eighteen and he and Anna were married in a small town in Alabama. It was the happiest day of Jason's life. He and Anna moved into a little shotgun house just outside town. The house was in a mill village and was very old. It was a one-bedroom house which they remodeled themselves, spending as much time in bed as they did working on the house. Anna even talked Jason into taking a job at the local cotton mill, and for her, he would do anything. He worked in the packing department and the first day on the job he spotted the sewing department with twenty-five girls who ran the machines. That would be enough to keep him there for a while.

Jason soon ran out of surplus money and started going out of town on weekends with Lenny, but five dollars from each game wasn't enough to build his bankroll back up and he missed Anna too much to concentrate on anything else. Anna soon became pregnant with their first child and her world was more beautiful than it had ever been. Unfortunately, Jason's urge to slip around with the girls hit him and he accepted an offer from one of the girls on the sewing line to get together for a little fun. He would work from three in the afternoon until eleven, and then he'd get up at seven a.m. to be at her house at eight sharp. Just minutes after her husband walked out the door for work. Somehow it seemed more exciting that way. The girl really wasn't that good in bed but Jason could make her scream so loud with pleasure that he had to cover her mouth to keep the neighbors from suspecting murder. Those screams fed his tremendous ego that would soon have to be fed every day. Jason later met the sister of this girl whom he wanted the minute he saw her as he did with all the girls lately. So now he was sleeping with the two sisters alone and sometimes together, and also a couple of the other girls at work.

The time Jason spent with Anna was getting less by the day and soon she never knew when he would be home or for how long. Lenny noticed the change and begged Jason to travel some and play the cons. Jason finally agreed, thinking, "Why not? All Anna does is bitch anyway."

Whenever Cecil was in town, he visited Jason. One evening during dinner at Jason's house, Cecil told him in private, "Jason, you've put yourself in a man's position and it's time you settle down and act like a husband and father." Jason said nothing for a minute then calmly replied with his usual cunning smile, "Hey Cecil, it's no problem. Anna understands that I need to play the cons."

Jason soon stopped visiting his father in prison and started to travel with Lenny regularly. He took a few trips with Cecil to meet people and learn some new games. Jason and Lenny were in Florida on Sunday night when Jason decided to call home. His first child was due in about three weeks so he wanted to stay in close touch. On the other end of the phone, he was told by Anna's sister that Anna had given birth to a baby girl. His sister-in-law was very rude to him about being so far away but Jason didn't care what she said, he had to be there to make money. Anna named the baby Elizabeth. Jason rushed home, made up with Anna, and decided to take Cecil's advice and settle down.

Jason had quit his job in the cotton mill so he decided to take another job at a metal factory. Soon he and Anna fought more than ever and Jason went back on the road for even longer trips. As time went by, Jason and Anna would break up and make up once a month. They accidentally had another daughter, Cindy. They both felt sure it would be a boy but one look at her and they decided another girl would be just fine.

Jason loved the kids and played with them all the time when he was home, but even they weren't enough to keep him home more than a couple of days each week. Anna just stayed home and was depressed all the time. She loved Jason with all her heart and didn't know what else she could do to capture his attention.

Anna spent lots of time writing letters to Jason's father and one day she got a letter back from him saying he'd be getting out of prison next month. He wanted to know if Jason would come out and pick him up. Jason was very excited and he and Cecil decided to drive out together to pick Frank up. Frank was very proud of Jason and his new family. He wished Christine could be there to see them. Anna took to Frank right away and ask him to live with them until he got back on his feet. Frank and Jason traveled together some but Jason wanted to run the con games and Frank wanted to gamble. Frank eventually decided to stay home with Anna and the kids while Jason was gone with Cecil and Lenny. Frank gambled in the local bars and roadhouses until he hit a winning streak and started drinking again. Jason talked to Frank about his drinking and Anna also begged him to stop.

She knew from conversations with Frank that he would never get past the death of Christine, and the drinking eased the pain. Jason took his father to visit Christine's grave, hoping it would shake his mind, but that seemed to make things worse. Then one day Jason called home and found Anna crying. She calmed down and told him, "Jason, please come home. There's been a shooting and your father is dead." Jason knew better than to try and get any details from her now, so he decided to wait until he got home to figure out what happened. He drove home and went straight to the bar where Frank was killed. Jason remembered Frank promising to never pick up another gun after the grocery store robbery. Jason knew everyone at the bar was lying to him about what had really happened with Frank. The next day Jason buried his father beside Christine and the baby.

Jason started hanging around town and sleeping with one of the girls who had worked at the bar. She quit her job after the shooting, and Jason knew something was wrong. She soon confessed that a guy named Blackie had shot Frank because Frank was drunk and wouldn't leave when asked. She said Blackie tried to force Frank out of the bar and Frank whipped him with his fists. Blackie then got a gun from the bar and shot Frank in the chest. Blackie told the story all different when the cops got there and everybody was afraid to disagree with him.

That night Jason lay quietly in his bed and thought about how his father had been killed. Frank was a drunk but it was his only way of dealing with Christine's death. Anna broke the silence saying, "Jason, are you okay?" "Yes, I found out today that this guy Blackie murdered Daddy. I'll see to it that he pays for this." Anna knew that there was no doubt that Blackie would have to pay but she dared not think of how.

I hardly know you and already

I say to myself,

Will she never understand?

How her person exalts all

That there is in me of

Blood and fire

Author unknown

5

After Frank's death, Jason spent most of his time on the road playing con games. He turned twenty-one that year and became obsessed with drag racing cars. He was spending all his money on the race cars and ignoring his family. It was the last straw for Anna. She went to him one afternoon while he was lying underneath a race car putting in a new clutch, and she said calmly, "Jason, I've called my sister and she's coming after me and the kids. I'm leaving you." He never acknowledged her. She wouldn't be gone long, he thought. But Anna must have been serious this time. She filed for divorce and never came back.

When Jason realized he had lost Anna, he sold his race car and started drinking heavily. Cecil knew that if Jason started drinking every day, he would end up just like Frank. He told Jason, "I've got a mark for you in Atlanta and I think you're ready for a big con. But you'll have to do this one on your own." Jason couldn't believe his ears. This would be his first real con game and he would be calling all the shots. Cecil told him, "I noticed that you liked that rent game you helped me with so here is the address to a realty company that I haven't played yet. Jason did not know much about Atlanta, but he had played this particular game with Cecil a few times and knew it well. His mind raced with thoughts of power and someday owning the City of Atlanta.

Lily

The next day Jason met with Lily, one of his regular girlfriends, who was a con artist herself. He explained her part in the game and she took off for Atlanta to set the stage. She was dressed in an expensive outfit that Jason had bought her, especially for this game. It was imperative that she look and act like a rich woman. He even borrowed a friend's brand new Nineteen Forty-Nine Cadillac for Lily to drive. She drove to the Empire Realty Company and met with a realtor there who drove her to a beautiful house about a quarter of a mile off the main road. Lily had told the realtor that the place she was looking for must be very private. When they arrived, she realized this place would be perfect. It was a large two-story with eighteen rooms on ten acres of land. The grounds were covered with flowers that were in bloom and the place was just beautiful.

Lily decided that no one could say 'no' to such a place. Lily explained to the realtor that she was an artist and needed to rent a quiet place to work on her paintings for three months.

The house was tied up in an estate and the owners thought it would be a great idea to rent it out for a while. Lily signed a contract for a three-month lease of the house and delivered the paperwork to Jason.

Rental House

Jason drove to Atlanta, and after seeing the house, he put an ad in the Atlanta newspaper which read:

LARGE EARLY AMERICAN HOME FOR LEASE OR RENT. EIGHTEEN ROOMS, BEAUTIFUL GARDENS. FOR MORE INFORMATION, PHONE WA-FOUR-ONE-FIVE-TWO AND ASK FOR NICKY.

The phone number in the ad was for a phone in an apartment Jason had rented for one month, posing as a government employee who was doing some classified work. The first call came that evening. It was a man and his wife who had just relocated to Atlanta and needed a place to stay until they could buy a house. Jason told the man that the house was still available, gave him directions to it and agreed to meet with him and his wife there the next afternoon to show it to them. Jason smiled with anticipation as he hung up the phone. His first big con was now underway.

Jason went out on the town that night and acted like a rich man. There were two girls coming on to him and he couldn't make up his mind which one he wanted to take home. So he ended up with both of them, and with the help of the white powder, it was an all-night party. He knew Atlanta was the town for him.

That next afternoon Jason met the couple at the house. They had arrived thirty minutes early to look around. Jason found them around back. He greeted them, introducing himself as Nicky Hale, the owner of the house. The man replied, "My name is Wendell Moore and this is my wife Brandi. We were looking around and we love this old place." Jason said, "It is a beautiful place, isn't it? My wife and I have lived here for the past three years. Very happily, I thought. However, she's divorced me. I'm stuck here with a huge house full of memories." Jason showed them the house inside, pausing at sentimental spots. The couple sympathized with his stories. When the tour was over, Jason told them, "The monthly rental will be three hundred dollars with a three hundred dollar deposit." The couple agreed readily. Jason drove to a nearby phone where he pulled out a business card and called his lawyer to come in and bring the lease. He actually called his apartment where Lenny was waiting for his cue. Lenny drove to the house dressed as the part of Jim Turner, Jason's lawyer. Introductions were conducted and Jason explained that the Moores wanted to lease the house for one year with an option to buy it. Lenny produced a contract and zipped through it while Jason milled around the house as though he was about to cry over losing his home.

Once Lenny got the six hundred dollars from the couple, Jason stepped in and said, "I'm sorry Mr. and Mrs. Moore, I failed to tell you earlier, the house won't be ready for you to move into for thirty days. The boxes you saw in the rooms upstairs are filled with my wife's personal things. She's left town for a while and her family has to come in and pick up those things. I'm afraid to touch anything of hers lately. If you could just bear with me this little bit of time, I'd really appreciate it." The couple was obviously disappointed, but the house was worth the wait. They agreed to the thirty-day wait. Lenny adjusted the move-in date on the contract and everyone put their initials next to th change. Jason shook their hands and as they left, he told them, "If you happen to drive by on Sunday to take another look at the house and see cars up here, it will be my wife's family. Please do not talk to them. They are all very unhappy with me. The house is yours in thirty days." They said good-bye and drove away.

Lenny and Jason complimented each other on their performance. Jason laughed at the way Lenny went through the contract. Lenny added, "Yeah, and I loved the way you almost went to pieces just remembering the past in this old house."

For the next thirty days, Jason and Lenny rented the house to as many people as they could in almost the same manner, cautioning each couple not to pay any attention to the cars coming in and out of the driveway. He didn't want any of them to stop while he was selling someone else. When the thirty days were up, Jason and Lenny had grossed four thousand dollars of which they paid Lily three hundred, covered other expenses and split the rest.

After getting a good night's sleep, Lenny packed his things and headed for Newnan but Jason simply couldn't leave the city. The city had become a drug to him. The women were the best, the restaurants the finest and with the money he was making, everybody called him Mr. Keeble. The city had won his soul. He wanted to wake up to it every day.

City of Atlanta

Jason found a much nicer apartment and started to build himself a fine wardrobe with the help of a young business woman whom he had met at the club. He learned to drink scotch whiskey and he snorted cocaine in the finest company money could buy. He had all but perfected six con games now and they were supporting him very well.

The war was over now and money was plentiful so Jason could find a sucker on every corner. He bought a new car, and as he drove down the streets of Atlanta it was as though it all belonged to him. Everything was going beautifully. He had money, women and the finest clothes when suddenly he was struck again. He met a blonde named Cheryl. She looked like she had just stepped out of some fashion magazine. She was twenty-five years old and worked for a real estate company that Jason had come in contact with during the set-up for one of his rent games. He forgot about renting the house when he saw her.

One week later Cheryl came to work and was met by a delivery boy with eleven roses and a card that read, "I hardly know you and already I say to myself---will she never understand how her person exalts all that there is in me of blood and fire. P.S. I'll meet you for lunch on Friday at MiMi's restaurant downtown." Cheryl was married and had been for seven years, had two daughters, a nice brick home and a lifestyle that was secure and boring. Jason had lit a fire in her heart and, in fact, she had thought of nothing but him since they first met. The rest of the week seemed to last a year. She went out and bought a new dress and made sure it showed off her nicely tanned legs. Jason wore a gray tailor-made suit with a white shirt, burgundy tie, gold collar bar, cuff links and a pair of handmade shoes from New York. His every hair was in place and his best manners had been refreshed the night before. In a way, Cheryl was like a con game to him so he'd play at his very best.

Cheryl Keeble

As Cheryl walked toward him in the lobby he was not surprised at how stunning she looked. He knew she was a class act from the very beginning. Once they were seated, the waitress delivered the twelfth rose in a vase. Cheryl smiled and said, "I wondered why you sent only eleven roses." Jason replied, "I kept the last one, betting that you would meet me today. A true lady can never resist roses." When Jason smiled, he was not only handsome but also confident. She thought, "I'm dying to take this man to bed." They both made small talk during the first drink.

She soon found herself so relaxed with his smooth style; it was as though they'd known each other for years. Jason was very playful and a happy-go-lucky type when he was with the girls and they all loved that quality in him. He spent much of their lunchtime making her laugh with his jokes and little stories. He charmed her through dessert and then suggested they take a walk. They left the restaurant and walked in the streets. It was a spring day and the wind blew through their hair. Cheryl thought, "If only we could walk forever." Finally, Jason took her hand and said, "Cheryl, I want to see you again tonight. I've thought about nothing but you ever since we met and after our lunch together, I feel as though I could take you away with me forever." Her heart skipped a beat wishing he would do just that. Then reality started setting in. Cheryl knew the truth had to come soon, so she told him, "Jason, I hope you won't be mad that I accepted your lunch date before telling you about myself. I'm married and have been for a long time. I've got two children so I can't just run out when I want to." It shook Jason but he was quick to notice she never said she wouldn't see him again. He smiled and replied, "It's no surprise to me to find a lady as beautiful as you married." He then reached into his jacket and produced a business card and added, "When you feel like slipping out, call me and we'll spend some time together."

Jason was good at getting answers from peoples' facial expressions and this lady's smile and slight blush said, "You can bet I'll call." He walked her to the car and as she drove away her heart was still pounding with the need to grab him and never let go. She looked at the card he'd given her which read, "Jason Alan Keeble, Independent Investor in Real Estate and Foreign Oil Leases." As she read the card, she thought, "What are you really like Mr. Jason Alan Keeble?" She knew she would think of nothing else until she found out.

Jason spent the next week playing penny ante cons and daydreaming about Cheryl. He hadn't noticed it but he was only making enough money to pay for his basic expenses. Had it not been for the extra money he had put away, he might have gotten desperate for cash. All he had on his mind was the beautiful blonde. Every day on the way to his apartment, he'd drive through her neighborhood and would think to himself, "I should just pull up to the door and carry her away." Then he'd drive home and lay awake most of the night with nothing but her on his mind.

It was Tuesday night when the phone rang at Jason's apartment. The female voice at the other end said, "Jason, its Cheryl. How are you doing?" "Fine," he smiled, "And how are you?" Their conversation was light, neither of the two saying anything with any meaning. Then suddenly Cheryl said, "Jason, I want to see you." The girl of Jason's dreams was getting closer all the time. Calmly Jason answered, "Cheryl, I've missed you. I want to see you too." Cheryl knew she didn't need an excuse to get near him and have him hold her in his arms, but she had one anyway and asked, "Jason, didn't you say you have a pool at your apartment?" "Yes," he answered. "Well," Cheryl continued, "I was thinking of coming over tonight for a swim if you don't already have plans." Jason considered for a minute that he had died and gone to heaven. He caught his breath and said to her, "I'll have the towels out and the pool lit up in ten minutes." She laughed and replied, "I'll put the kids to bed and be there in an hour." As they hung up the phone, Cheryl thought, "I should not sound as easy around him as I really am."

When Cheryl arrived, Jason could hold back no longer. As he took her hand, he politely kissed her on the cheek. She stood there speechless and Jason simply smiled and pointed her towards the bathroom saying, "You can get dressed in there." As she walked from the bathroom in her swimsuit, their eyes met, each wondering what the other thought. Jason's mind was spinning around. "What a beautiful woman," he thought. Her body was thin, her skin well-tanned and her lines and curves were all perfect. Her legs were firm and long, her waist was small and her breasts were just big enough to compliment her long shiny blonde hair. When they got to the pool, Jason took off his robe and Cheryl could see his tanned body very well as he stood near the bright pool lights. He had a strong muscular body. Cheryl couldn't look at his chest without becoming embarrassed. In her eyes he was gorgeous but she didn't want to stare. It was safer to look at his eyes. They stared into each other's eyes and seemed to be glued together with neither one wanting to move. Jason finally asked, "Shall we swim?" They swam for an hour, playing and laughing as though they were kids. Jason was careful not to touch her other than brushing against her or grabbing her hand to stop her from splashing water in his face. He was in fact, a perfect gentleman, keeping the evening moving smoothly.

Eventually, Cheryl had to go so they walked back to his apartment to change her clothes. While she was standing in his bedroom changing, he was wondering if he should try to kiss her. She walked out of the bedroom in her silk dress and said to Jason, "Well, I guess I need to leave. It's getting late." She walked toward him and he told himself that another kiss on the cheek was acceptable. As he pulled her toward him, they fell deep into each other's arms and into a soft passionate kiss. Then suddenly Cheryl felt herself getting very weak. She felt a stirring and knew she was becoming aroused much too fast. She pulled away and said, "Jason, I must go." Jason released her and replied, "I understand. I only hope you'll want to visit me again soon." She explained to him that it was nothing he'd done, she just needed to get home. The next day Jason sent another eleven yellow roses to her job. The card read, "To Blondie, my favorite swim partner." She read the card and thought, "This man is almost too good to be true."

That night when Jason got home, he found a note on his door that read, "Stopped by to get my twelfth rose but you were out. Meet me at MiMi's on Friday night at seven p.m." The note was signed, "Love 'n stuff, Cheryl."

One month after their first real date, Cheryl called Jason from a hotel room in Daytona Beach Florida to say that she was asking her husband for a divorce and that she missed their swims together very much. The next week her husband moved out of the house and a month later their divorce was finalized. By now, she and Jason were dating hot and heavy, so she asked Jason to move in with her and the kids. Six months later they were married quietly. Jason was deeply in love.

Jason and Cheryl's Home

Cheryl's family and neighbors did not care much for Jason and weren't sure that he and Cheryl were really married, so Jason decided they would move. The new house was a mansion in a beautiful section on the south side of Atlanta and the nearest neighbor was three miles away. Cheryl had found the house and when she showed it to Jason, he could see how much she loved it, so, he decided to buy it. It was the first time he had ever applied for credit but with the large down payment he had, the loan went right through. The house was a large two story with a carport attached to the side. Two old oaks stood in the front yard and the entire house was complimented by flowers of all types. It sat off the main highway, about five hundred feet, had a large horseshoe-shaped driveway with a split rail fence and yellow roses that covered the fence when they were in bloom. Cheryl spent the next year decorating the inside of the house. Her children had taken to Jason very well. He seemed to work magic with children and never got upset with them. Occasionally he would have his own two daughters spend weekends with them in the new house, which made him feel good because he had neglected his daughters a lot since his divorce from Anna.

At first, Cheryl accepted Jason's kids well. Then she began to show resentment toward their being there. She said they just didn't have the manners of her own children. That really didn't sit well with Jason but he was determined to make this marriage work. He didn't bring his kids to the house again but instead, took them for a visit with Cecil and Lynn.

Cheryl really didn't know much about Jason's job, except that he traveled a lot. He told her he had decided to take a job that would allow him to spend more time at home. He took a job selling diesel trucks. There was some travel involved but only overnight and with Jason's latest vow to himself to settle down and go straight, this job would be just fine. He met a lot of people on the job who had plenty of money and he couldn't help but spot the greedy ones and think, "I could take this guy for all he's got but that's all behind me now." He did, however, stash special names in the back of his wallet just in case times were to get hard.

Jason and Cheryl truly loved each other and when it was just the two of them at home, all was great. Then one night Jason stopped by a nightclub called the Fireplace. He had spent a lot of time there since he had lived in Atlanta. He intended only to see a few of his friends and be on his way, but when he spoke to Fran, a hostess, he noticed she seemed very troubled. When he got her to talk about it, she said, "That creep by the dance floor with the gray suit on is driving me crazy to spend the night with him. He offered me fifty dollars to go over to my house for a good time. He's disgusting to me." Jason thought for a minute and the old con man came out of him. Without hesitation, he told Fran, "Look, Franny, play up to him and try to see his money roll." "You must be crazy." She replied. "No Fran," Jason said. "Listen to me. You make sure he's got plenty of money then tell him you'll let him spend the night at your house. Give him the business that you got pinched a couple of weeks ago and you thought he might be another cop. I'll show you how to make this a fun night." Jason smiled his little sly smile and walked away. Fran knew he wouldn't double cross her so she agreed and played along with the scam. When Fran gave Jason the signal that the guy had money with him, Jason got Fran's spare key and left the bar.

After work, Fran let the sucker follow her home. She poured him a glass of wine and led him into her bedroom, where she started kissing him and undressing him and throwing his clothes onto a chair. Suddenly Jason bounced out of the bedroom closet holding a gun which he pointed at them both. Fran screamed. The sucker fell to his knees on the floor, begging Jason not to kill him. Jason then took the guy's wallet from his pants on the chair, dumped out Fran's purse, took her money and jumped out the bedroom window. Fran ran straight to the phone.

The sucker yelled, "What are you doing?" "I'm calling the police stupid. What does it look like? We've been robbed and there's no telling what else he took before we got here." The guy stopped her saying, "Look, lady, I'm married and can't stand for the police to get involved in this, so please don't call them." He started pulling his clothes back on while Fran argued and dialed the phone. After the sucker ran out the door, Fran hung up the phone. Later that night, Jason came back and split the sucker's money with her. They had sex and Jason drove home.

The next night instead of going home, Jason made a fast trip to a friend's house and picked up four grams of cocaine. He went straight to the Fireplace nightclub and slipped in through the back door. He told one of the girls what he had and she rushed him and his goodies into the ladies restroom. He sat the package on the sink, then using a razor blade and a mirror that he kept in his car, he cut out several lines of cocaine. The waitress left him there and when each of the girls would get a break from their tables, they would go to the restroom for a line of the coke. Jason was soon sailing on the coke and when the ladies who were customers at the club would drift into the room, they could hardly believe their eyes. There sat Jason in the ladies room who seemed to think he was supposed to be there. Crazier still, no one seemed to mind. Before the night was over, they all got used to him and just took care of business and got out. He did invite a few of them to snort a little coke with him.

Jason spent the rest of the night there, snorting coke and drinking scotch whiskey, and when he drove home the next morning at six a.m., Cheryl met him at the door yelling and throwing things. He knew he could never put up with her bitching without slapping her so he told her, "Look, Cheryl, when I come home from drinking you leave me the hell alone and when I've had some sleep we'll have these little quiz shows." Cheryl could see in his eyes that he could be dangerous if need be, and never again did she argue with him when he was drinking. When he woke up that evening he wouldn't say much about why he got drunk. He showered and rushed out of the house to work.

Soon Jason started to hang in the club every night and he eventually quit his job. He told Cheryl he would be out of town for a few days and without another explanation, he picked up Lenny and they left for Fort Lauderdale, Florida where they spent the next fifteen days playing con games. When Jason came home Cheryl was calm and asked him to tell her where he'd been for so long. After showing her the three thousand dollars he had made, he told her, "Cheryl, when I met you, I fell in love with you at once. I neglected to tell you about myself and what I really do for a living, but now it's only fair that you know the truth. The business card I gave you about real estate and oil leases was a fake. I'm a con man and have been all my life. I took the job selling trucks to be with you more and now I must tell you that I won't be working that job anymore." Cheryl cried for two days and barely ate. She had truly counted on Jason being "Mr. Perfect."

"I'm a con artist in that I'm an actor. I make people believe something is real when they know perfectly well it isn't."

John Lithgow

6

The country's economy was getting better with each year. By Nineteen Fifty-One, the majority of middle-class America owned cars, bought houses and took long vacations. With money more available, the con games were better than ever.

Jason telling Cheryl about his life as a con man was a big mistake. She threatened to take the children and leave him each time he went out on the road. Time passed with Jason doing nothing but traveling and playing the cons. Finally, Cheryl tried to convince him that by putting himself in jeopardy with the law and maybe even being killed, he would leave his kids with no father and her kids would be devastated. Eventually, this led to a final ultimatum by Cheryl. She tried to keep Jason home with lots of sex and good home cooking. She even taught the kids to beg him not to go. As usual, Cheryl finally talked Jason into trying the straight life one more time.

Jason had moved into an extra bedroom in the basement so they spent a Saturday putting his things back into Cheryl's bedroom. The next day he went to interview for a "real" job. There was an ad in the paper for an assistant manager at a local loan company. Jason thought, "This might be a good job for me." The manager was a young guy who needed help with collecting money from the customers. The guy immediately liked Jason. The job sounded fine but the salary was less than one dollar per hour, which was about half the salary Jason should be getting. Jason knew he couldn't live on that kind of money. He told the guy he wouldn't take the job, thanked the guy and left. As he was leaving, the manager followed him outside, telling him discretely, "I need some help badly and I think you and I can help each other. I know the pay is lousy but if you'll take the job and listen to what I tell you, I'll show you how to skim enough money off the company to keep you going." Jason saw just enough greed in the man to whet his appetite and decided to give it a try. Once back home, Jason announced to Cheryl, "I am now the new assistant manager of the Hometown Loan Company. I will try my best to hold down this job if that's what it takes to make you happy." Cheryl was more content now than she had been in a long time and knew things would be better for her and Jason.

The manager at the loan company was Larry Hayes. Jason was on target about the guy's greed and they worked together well. He showed Jason some tricks in the finance business and in return, Jason introduced him to some of the hottest girls in town. Jason soon learned to make his collection job a con game, telling the customers all sorts of stories in order to get them to pay. Word soon got around about Jason's ability to collect money which no one else had any success with. Soon other companies offered him jobs with good salaries, but he was happy right where he was. With Cheryl not knowing about any of the extra money he was making, he had plenty of money left over for his other habits. Jason would make false loans at his office for himself and then pay the money back by changing payment dates on other people's loans and keeping their late charges to pay his own loan payment. He couldn't resist playing small con games while he was out working on his job. A year passed and things at the Keeble house were just fine. Jason would often say he had late night collections to make, giving him time for the clubs and the girls.

A few months later, Jason's boss Larry decided to transfer to another company for more money, leaving Jason the newly promoted manager. Larry drove a Nineteen Fifty-Two Packard Patrician Four Hundred sedan which Jason wanted more than any car he had ever seen. The car was a beautiful white with black interior and had all the extras possible. He had fallen in love with that car from the first day he had seen it and had made Larry promise that if he ever sold it, Jason would have first dibs on it. When Larry left, he told Jason, "The car is yours for fifteen hundred dollars. My girlfriend has two cars so I won't need this one anymore."

Jason was ecstatic. When he told Cheryl he was going to get the car she tried to burst his bubble, telling him they couldn't afford it. She knew having a car like that would only make him want the old life more. But she shouldn't have told him he couldn't afford the car. He wasn't used to hearing the word no. The next day he made a loan at the bank for the car. He and Cheryl argued and she yelled about the car all night. She insisted he take it back but when she finally drove it, the magic rubbed off on her and she was quite proud to be seen in it.

Jason knew he would need extra money to pay the car payments so he put a plan together. He called Lenny and told him of his scheme while they were having drinks. On Monday morning, Jason looked through the local obituaries and selected the name of a man who had lived in an area he knew to be a prominent section of town. With his knowledge of finance and a good friend at the credit bureau office, Jason was able to obtain the deceased man's social security number. He then ran a check on the guy's credit and found it was in very good standing at the time of his demise. Jason then called Lenny and gave him the information. Lenny went to a man he knew who made false driver's licenses and Lenny soon became Mr. James Hollis Treadwell, alive and in sudden need of a loan.

Lenny as an older man

Lenny, posing as Treadwell, showed up at Jason's finance office that evening and Jason had his secretary Brenda take a loan application on him. Brenda came to Jason with the application and said, "Jason, this man's credit is perfect according to the credit bureau. I just wonder why he'd come to us for a loan and not use his own bank." Jason looked the application over and told Brenda, "It's probably for a gambling debt or a girlfriend and he's keeping it from his wife." The credit bureau would take about ten days to show the guy as being deceased and that evening the loan was made. When Jason made the loan he changed the dates on the contract to make it look like the guy had been in and made the loan just two days before his death. Brenda checked the guy's driver's license and gave him the check. She never noticed the change of dates on the contract.

Jason and Lenny made about ten such loans after that, using friends of Lenny's for each loan. After they split the money, Jason had enough left to completely pay his car off and stick back the rest for a rainy day. When the payments came due on the loans Jason made to Mr. Treadwell and the others, Brenda called the customers' houses only to find out they had passed away. Jason would then file an insurance claim on them and let the insurance company reimburse the finance company. Brenda soon saw what Jason was doing but she never told anyone, which later paid off for her. That little con kept Cheryl off Jason's back about the payments on his car.

Six months after Jason became manager of the finance company, a local car dealer who Larry had introduced him to started to offer him little kick-backs in exchange for making loans on cars for people who had really poor credit. Things were going well for Jason until a local recruiting agency asked him to come in and interview for a position as a business manager at an automobile dealership. The guy painted Jason a very pretty picture and guaranteed Jason that he could triple his present salary. Jason thought it over but really didn't want to leave his little gold mine. It would, however, be a good time to push the supervisor for a raise. Jason telephoned his supervisor about the job offer and told him that he liked the finance business and would stay on for a one hundred dollar a month raise. The supervisor replied, "Jason, this company wouldn't give you a hundred dollar a month raise if your life depended on it. You know this is an easy job and besides, we've got guys begging every day to work here for less than you make now." The phone was silent for a moment then the supervisor continued, "Jason, be sure to get your monthly report in on time this month and I'll see you next Thursday." The phone went dead and Jason just sat there a minute staring at the floor.

That night Jason was very restless. Cheryl questioned him, "Is everything alright Jason?" After a long pause, he answered, "It's my supervisor at work. He hurt my feelings today about a raise I asked for and now he's going to pay for it. Nobody treats me like that." Cheryl suddenly felt threatened that their little dream house might fall down. She knew that Jason didn't like people who tried to push him around. She also knew Jason would surely retaliate in some way.

The next week Jason decided to take the job in Atlanta at the automobile dealership and told his new boss he needed a week to give notice to the loan company. Cheryl was pleased with his decision to take a better job and the money was much better. She was very glad that he wasn't mad enough to go back out on the road playing the cons.

On Monday Jason called Lenny and asked him to drive over to an old section of town called "Cabbage Town" where he picked up nine winos. He drove them, one at a time, to Jason's loan office where Jason made them each a loan for one thousand dollars. Lenny took them to the local bank to cash the checks. He paid each of them fifty dollars which was enough to buy wine for a week. That little deal netted Jason and Lenny eight thousand five hundred and fifty dollars. They split that fifty/fifty as usual.

The next day Jason resigned, neglecting to contact his supervisor with a notice. On his way out he gave Brenda five hundred dollars and said, "Tell them whatever it takes to keep your job." He then put the balance of the money he had taken into a bank account he had set up for his daughters, which Cheryl knew nothing about. The supervisor at the loan company found all the bad loans sometime later, figuring out what Jason had done. Brenda said she knew nothing of the wrongdoings but was glad Jason was gone. That saved her job. The supervisor knew the weight would inevitability fall on himself for poor supervision so he wrote off the uncollectable loans and never mentioned the episode to his main office.

One week later Jason took the train to Chicago to attend a crash course for his new job. Cheryl boasted to her family and friends that Jason would soon be a "Business Manager." She thought to herself, "He's really settled down now. He's a good husband." Little did she know that Jason had been playing con games in Chicago for the entire three weeks he was there and profits were rolling in. Lenny had taken the train to meet Jason to help him and they were making plenty of money while enjoying the girls and the food.

Toward the end of the second week of Jason's stay in Chicago, he called home to check on Cheryl and the kids. She started crying and said, "Jason, this idiot hit your car yesterday and since he knew the cops, they didn't even make a case against him." The car was Jason's pride and joy. Even though it made him sick to his stomach, he pretended that it didn't matter. He didn't want Cheryl to be upset. When he got home, he would simply buy another car. A much nicer one.

Jason soon started his new job and found out he had a lot of paper work that he hadn't counted on. His job was to get the new customers to finance their car through the dealership plan. In turn, the dealership made large premiums from the banks who furnished the money. All day Jason was up and down with applications for credit and trying to get some bank to finance the deal. Except for the people who had no money, it was exciting to see how easily he could talk people into doing what he wanted them to do. He was able to con the banks and loan companies into handling loans that no one else would touch. Then one night he was at the nightclub when he overheard a guy saying he could get anyone financed on a car, regardless of how bad their credit was. They had a drink and the guy explained to Jason that the dealer he worked for was co-signing with the customers who had bad credit as long as they brought large down payments.

Customers who had terrible credit came to Jason and he would tell them, "I can't get your car financed here but it might be that a friend of mine can help you." After he explained, he would get them to agree to pay him one hundred dollars for his help. He gave them directions to his friend's place. He then called the friend to tell him the customers were coming. The friend met the customers at the door with the red carpet treatment. They would buy a new car at list price and were financed on the spot. The salesman paid Jason a twenty-five dollar finder's fee for each customer and that along with the one hundred Jason had already charged the customer, made him six or seven hundred more per month that he didn't have to tell Cheryl about.

Things were going pretty well for Jason. He could wheel and deal and still keep Cheryl happy and at home. Then one day a friend of Cecil's came to visit him with plans to make them a lot of money. The guy would pose as a businessman who was opening a new tire recapping business. It was near completion when his wife left him and took all the money that was in their bank account. He would lose all if some financial support didn't come along. Jason had lots of names of people who were saving for the down payment on a car. He had contracts printed and visited the people to explain the opportunity to invest their money and get big cash returns in six months. He drove them one by one to the building that the guy had rented and set up for the game. Jason could hardly believe how quick they jumped at the deal.

The six months passed and the con man settled up with Jason and left town. Jason told the people he was to be paid a fee for helping get the investors and that the guy had cheated everyone out of their money. The police were called by one of the investors and Jason was almost indicted by the district attorney. He finally got out of it by producing the contract that said he would be paid a fee at the end of the six months just like everyone else. That left the cops with no case. Jason told them all he could about the guy and left it to them to find him. On Monday, he was asked to leave his job when his manager got wind of the investigation. He told Cheryl about the deal and led her to believe that he thought the guy was sincere and he'd messed everything up but Cheryl somehow knew the truth. They wound up in a big fight ending with Jason telling Cheryl that he would never be what she wanted him to be. Jason handed her one thousand dollars he made from the scam and told her, "Cheryl, take this money and make a new life for yourself. I'm leaving town and I won't be back."

Be Yourself
Everyone else is already taken

Oscar Wilde

"Better a diamond with a flaw
than a pebble without."

Confucius

7

Jason spent the next three months in Florida playing con games and trying to sort out in his mind what he wanted to do about his relationship with Cheryl. He truly loved her and the kids but the straight life just didn't seem to work for him. Cecil played poker in Florida a lot so he stayed in touch with Jason to make sure he was okay. One evening when they were together, a friend of Cecil's told them of a gemstone that appeared to be a flawless diamond. The difference between this stone and a real diamond were such that it could pass any test available to the common person to be very real. He told Cecil he had three cases full of these stones for sale. A thought suddenly hit Jason as he headed back to his hotel that night and he said to himself, "There's an old debt I owe...and I think I've figured out how to repay it." He bought the fake diamonds and put them in the trunk of his car.

Lenny knew the guy Blackie, who had killed Jason's father, and talked to him often enough to keep up with his shady deals. Blackie owned a bar now and bought stolen items as a fence. When Jason explained to Lenny what he wanted to do, Lenny laughed out loud and quickly agreed to help. They drove back to Newnan that night.

The next day Lenny pulled Blackie to a rough section of town to talk to him about some hot televisions he had access to. As they talked, a dark sedan pulled up to the red light and stalled. A clean-cut gentleman stepped out of the car and raised the hood. He wore a suit which made him stick out in that part of town but stranger than the suit was the briefcase handcuffed to his wrist. He struggled under the hood for a while, the briefcase getting in his way. As Lenny and Blackie talked,

Lenny couldn't keep his eyes off the guy with the briefcase. Suddenly the guy took a key from his pocket and uncuffed the briefcase from his hand, sat it on the fender and continued working on the car. All of a sudden Lenny broke into a run, grabbed the briefcase and ran down the street. The man chased him, yelling for him to stop. When the man came back toward his car he saw Blackie and approaching him said, "Excuse me sir but that kid grabbed my case. Can you help me find him?" Blackie responded calmly, "I didn't see anything." "But sir," the guy continued, "please let me explain, the case is filled with marked diamonds. They are useless to him. If he tries to sell them he'll be caught. I was delivering them to a local jeweler and I'll lose my job if I can't get them back. Please take my card and if you could get them back, I'll pay you a thousand dollars reward."

Two days later Lenny went back to see Blackie again about the stolen televisions. Blackie told him about his visit with the guy with the briefcase and how he knew what was in the case. Lenny boasted, "That case was full of diamonds." Blackie replied, "I know it was diamonds but there's a problem. They are marked and if you try to sell them, you'll go straight to jail. The guy offered me a five hundred dollar reward to get the case back so I'll take the case to him and we'll split the money." "Bullshit," Lenny argued. "I had those stones checked and there's about one hundred thousand dollars worth of diamonds in that case." Blackie laughed and said, "Ok kid, bring the case to me and we might be able to make a better deal."

When Blackie saw the stones, sweat started popping out on his forehead from greed and Lenny loved it. Blackie said, "I'll give you one thousand dollars for the case." Lenny laughed and replied, "You must be crazy. I told you, I know what those stones are worth." So did Blackie but he wasn't going to tell Lenny. Blackie figured the case for about one hundred and fifty thousand dollars. He could send them to a friend and have them recut and mounted. Finally, Lenny said, "Look, if you want the case for twenty-five thousand, it's yours, but not a penny less." They argued for a while before Blackie finally gave in and bought the stones.

Lenny and Jason laughed at Blackie, knowing he had bought a case full of fake diamonds. Jason knew he was still far from even with Blackie but this was a good start. The next week Blackie was told the diamonds were worthless and he was furious. Having no thought of Jason being involved, he went after Lenny. That night Lenny's girlfriend called Jason and said, "Jason, I'm at the county hospital. Lenny has been beaten up very badly and he's asking for you. Will you please come over?" Jason rushed to Lenny's room and Lenny whispered to him, "Jason, it was Blackie and he says he'll kill me if I don't get his money back to him in one week." Jason replied, "Don't worry partner, I'll take care of him. You just get well." Jason called on some guys he knew from Atlanta and they followed Blackie home, busted his head with a ball bat and drove him to a deserted country road where Jason waited. As Blackie regained consciousness, Jason stood over him and said, "Blackie, you look scared like an animal and I'm sure that's the way you looked the night you killed my father. I'm the one who put the fake diamonds on you and now you put Lenny in the hospital. That, my friend, was a terrible mistake for you." Blackie cried to him. "It wasn't me who jumped on Lenny and I told you what happened with your father."

Jason dropped down to one knee so he would be eye to eye with Blackie and holding him by his hair said, "You're a stinking liar and a scum bag." One of the guys with Jason pointed a shotgun at Blackie, letting it rest against his cheek. Jason then said, "Now, you tell me the truth about my father or I'll have this guy blow your brains out." Blackie cried and told Jason, "Your father and I were drunk. We got into a fight. I was mad and got carried away. I shot him and I'm sorry. Please forgive me. I'll give you money or anything you want." Jason then asked the guy with the gun to step back. He held Blackie up by his hair saying, "You made a big mistake killing my father and now it's payday but not with your money. Don't cry and beg." The guy with the shotgun then walked over to Blackie and shot him in the face, almost removing his head. As Jason got into his car he thought, "The debt is paid now, Daddy."

One lie is enough to question all truths.

Anonymous

8

Cheryl had been separated from Jason for several months, but the fact remained that she loved him very much. She visited him at the boarding house he had moved into and convinced him to move back into the house with her, but this time he made the rules and they were simple. No restrictions on his life. At first, he was only gone when a friend invited him to play a con game that was out of town, but then he started to hang in the nightclubs again until two and three o'clock in the morning. Cheryl thought it was simply his way of saying he didn't want her anymore but the truth remained that Jason had become addicted to the nightlife and the girls.

Jason was very close to all the girls who worked at the club, especially Cindy. Whenever he saw a girl he wanted to meet, he'd dance with her once then cue Cindy to make her move. Cindy would mention to the girl that Jason was wealthy and a sucker for a pretty face. The girl would most times, automatically come on to him, all smiles. Jason was quick to pick up on a person who was gullible or might be a mark for his con games. On this particular night, the girl was for sure ready to spend some money.

Jason had danced with her but when Cindy mentioned he was rich; it didn't seem to phase her. He asked Cindy to look in the coat closet and get any personal information from the girl's wallet in her purse. Cindy was able to get the girl's name, address, and social security number. In the meantime, he charmed her and they ended up leaving the club and going to an all-night diner to have some breakfast. As their night ended, Jason drove her back to her car and made no effort to even kiss her.

The next day he got a friend to run the girl's social security number through the credit bureau. He found out she was the wife of a very wealthy businessman in North Atlanta who traveled most of the time. Her name was Yvonne Thompson. The next week Jason called Yvonne and invited her to meet him at the club for drinks. After a drink and some small talk, they went to an expensive dinner club. Jason stopped at a service station to use the restroom and while he was inside, Yvonne noticed the clutter of papers on the dash of his car. Curiosity got the best of her as Jason hoped it would and she glanced over some of the papers. They were contracts and they appeared to be business deals that Jason was making in real estate. The figures on the documents averaged around one hundred thousand dollars. She rummaged some more and found a checkbook that showed him writing checks for very large amounts. It was all very impressive to Yvonne as Jason was certainly her kind of man.

After dating Yvonne a few times, Jason went to meet her one night, acting as though the world had dealt him all the wrong cards. Yvonne asked, "Jason. What is the matter? You're always so cheerful and now you look so sad." Without raising his head, Jason replied, "It's nothing." After some coaxing from Yvonne, he confessed, "Today I got this hot tip from a friend who owns a big real estate company. He says this company from out of town is going to be buying a tract of land in town soon and he knows which one they want. I can buy the land now for thirty thousand dollars and sell it to them in six months for at least one hundred thousand. The problem is the bank. They don't want to let me have all the money." Jason then quickly changed the subject but before the night ended, Yvonne begged Jason to let her in on the deal and she would put up twenty of the thirty thousand dollars. Jason told her in great detail how the deal was a good one but she'd be wise to think it over first. She insisted they make the purchase the very next day.

As the months passed, Yvonne bought Jason some new clothes and a gold bracelet. In turn, Jason taught her some tricks about sex and introduced her to the great white powder. Cocaine. They came very close to getting caught in bed together at her house by Yvonne's husband but somehow that seemed very exciting to Jason. Each time he gave Yvonne an update on the land deal it only made her want him more. She'd show her husband that she could make money on her own. Then the time came for the land to be sold to the big company, but Jason called Yvonne and told her that they must meet at once. Jason showed up at the meeting in an old rough Ford car. He was unshaven, in jeans and red-eyed. As he drove her in the old car to the tract of land, Jason did not speak one single word. He seemed to be in some kind of trance. Once they arrived, he explained to Yvonne that the land they had bought had developed a sinkhole in it, so the deal was lost. The bank, he told her, had foreclosed on him and took all he had worked for. After a while, he produced a pistol and talked about taking his life, but Yvonne stopped him. Trying to lighten a tremendous load of guilt he bore, she didn't dare mention her loss of twenty thousand dollars.

As Jason drove home he thought, "Yvonne took all that very well and after my expenses, I still cleared about fifteen thousand dollars. Cheryl and I can spend some time together now." His con abilities were getting better each day, which meant that he and Cheryl could live well on all the money he'd soon earn.

With slouch and swing around the ring

We trod the Fool's Parade!

We did not care; we knew we were

The Devil's Own Brigade;

And shaven head and feet of lead

Make a merry masquerade.

Oscar Wilde

9

In the latter part of Nineteen Fifty-Three, Jason bought a new house for his family. His biological children started visiting again on weekends and everybody got along fine. Money was plentiful now, keeping Jason at home a lot more. Cheryl had ceased hassling him about his lifestyle and the new house seemed to make her very happy.

Jason's friends respected him a great deal. They could go to him at any time for help and advice. One Sunday Lenny visited, spending the entire day alone with Jason in the study. Lenny had made a connection in South America to transport cocaine into the country but had no means of distributing the drugs. After listening to Lenny, Jason explained to him that he had no experience with drugs other than his occasional use. Lenny pleaded with Jason for his help in having a business of his own and Jason reluctantly agreed to help Lenny by supplying people to sell the drugs on the streets.

Jason visited people he knew and trusted, from which he hand-picked a few to sell the drugs. He would be the supplier and no drugs would be brought into his house. In return, Jason got fifty percent of all the action. Lenny spent all of his time traveling back and forth to South America by boat delivering the drugs to Jason. Within three months the business had grown to proportions beyond both their dreams.

Although Jason had very little involvement with drugs, his name leaked out to street punks, dope addicts and dealers. Some became violently jealous of his quick success and power. Threats were made on his life, forcing him to hire a bodyguard. Cheryl could tell that there were problems and it wasn't just a con game this time but she also knew that she could do nothing to stop him.

Soon Jason had drugs in every nightclub and on every street corner in Atlanta. He employed twenty people plus several street runners. He also supplied some prostitutes he knew with cocaine, and they, in turn, sold some drugs for him.

He had personal tailors and bought clothes for himself that were shipped in from Paris. Life was very good, then suddenly Cheryl became pregnant which thrilled Jason more than anything that had ever happened in his life. He thought to himself, "Lord, let it be a son. I need one right now."

The problems with the drug business demanded more and more of Jason's time now. What happened to the simple life of a con man? His street corner drug dealers started getting robbed in broad daylight. It seemed to Jason that penny-ante street punks were destroying his operation, making him look like a fool. Somehow he knew these robberies were set up by rival gangs. If this operation was to continue, Jason would have to get more involved. He declared war on the gang from the North side of Atlanta that was causing the trouble. Every day brought bloodshed to some of his now fifty henchmen. Lenny and Jason agreed to fight this thing to the finish.

Jason didn't know it, but Lenny was now strung out on coke. He had to have it every day. He paid a friend to take his boat to South America and transport the coke back while he was hiding out with one of his favorite girlfriends.

The FBI had long been watching the operation but couldn't find out who the kingpin was. All the people who worked for Jason were loyal to him, keeping their mouths shut when they were questioned. All the feds could do was wait for someone to make a mistake.

Two months later, as Jason lay in front of the television with the kids, Cheryl told him the time had come for the baby. Jason and his bodyguards transported her to the hospital. The bodyguards were a precaution that Jason felt was very necessary and everyone in his family had to be escorted any place they went. He wanted to be extra careful that nothing happened to this new baby.

Cheryl was always embarrassed by the bodyguards. The kids at school asked all kinds of questions about the long black cars that brought Jason's kids to school every day.

Cheryl's labor was difficult for a third child and lasted almost eight hours. On September twenty-seventh, Ninteen Fifty-Three, a baby boy was born. Jason and Cheryl named him James Alan Keeble. The boy's eyes were blue and looked like Cheryl's but the rest of his body was identical to his father's. Jason was very proud of his new son and spent time at home with him that he really needed to devote to his now ever-demanding drug business.

Three months later, Cheryl became pregnant again. When Jason heard the news he was overjoyed. Cheryl showed no excitement and when Jason questioned her, she simply said, "Jason, I've got three children now and no means of supporting them except you. I know that the way you are living your life now you'll end up dead or in some prison and I can't manage this family alone." Those words hit him so hard he couldn't even answer her. The next day she was driven to a private doctor that Jason kept on the payroll for things he didn't want to report during these gang wars and an abortion was performed on her. A couple of days later, Jason met Cheryl at a nearby diner where they ate lunch and agreed to never talk about the ordeal again.

Soon Jason owned interests in all types of businesses. People used their homes and businesses as security to get drugs from him. They would sell the drugs and make large profits. As time went by, they'd use more drugs than they sold and consequently, Jason would end up with their businesses or homes. The drug wars raged on. It all seemed so stupid to Jason. He hated violence but all the meetings he attended with his rivals would end with nothing settled. The families of Jason's henchmen were affected, children were killed, cars were bombed and no end seemed to be in sight. Jason had a lawyer, Jack Hunter, who was one of the most trusted people in the organization. Jack's loyalties to Jason grew stronger each year. Jason depended on Jack greatly to hide all the drug money in various accounts, making Jason look like a real estate investor.

Jack Hunter's son was being accepted into a private college to study medicine. Two weeks after he started, word got back to Jack that his son had been thrown out of school. When Jack stormed into the dean's office, he was told, "Mr. Hunter, your son would become a fine doctor but the reputation you have is one that we will not have associated with this college." Jack's love and concern for his son were about to force him to make some decisions he never thought he would have to make. The dean told him that if he could clear his reputation and change his lifestyle, they would allow his son to come back to the college. There was no more to think about. He owed this to his son. Hunter decided to step forward and clear his family name. He showed up at the local district attorney's office with a list of things the grand jury would want to hear. He was quickly rushed to the head office of the FBI and a full statement was taken.

Everything looked promising for a conviction of Jason and Lenny. The inspector asked Hunter, "Why, Jack, would you, of all people, want to testify against Jason Keeble and Lenny Patillo?" Jack's answer was simple, "I want to clear my name." The inspector told Jack, "Your life can't be worth a match when this news hits the streets. But I'll do all I can to protect you." Jack replied, "I know exactly what I'm doing and I'll appreciate your help." Hunter knew the moment he went into protective custody, Jason would be alerted and close up the operation. The feds wanted Jason so badly they agreed to let Hunter remain active in the organization. As Hunter watched the agents gloat over the thought of busting Jason Keeble, he knew that because of Jason's ability with the cons and being a shrewd businessman, the end result would only embarrass the FBI.

Lenny organized one of his bigger cocaine deliveries that next night, so he decided to handle it himself. Hunter had no idea that Lenny would be

THE MASTER OF HIS GAME

there since he had been letting someone else make his connections. FBI agents were there and arrested Lenny. Jason knew there was a rat but wasn't sure where to look for him. Then Jason got a call from the police station where he had a rookie cop on his payroll. The rookie cop informed Jason it was Hunter who had signed the statement. Jason refused to believe him and it wasn't until Jason demanded that he and the cop meet, and he saw a copy of the statement that he believed who it was. Of all people, Jason never thought Hunter could do such a thing. There must have been a great deal of pressure on him. Or he'd lost his mind.

That next week Jason and Hunter met. Jason spoke to Hunter about the problem as if he didn't know Hunter was to blame, asking that Hunter help find the rat. When the meeting was over, Hunter was sure that his name had never gotten to Jason and all would be well until Jason was arrested. Then Hunter would take a new name and move out of the country. That night, Hunter got a call from a realtor in New York that Jason had been dealing with concerning some warehouse space. Hunter knew that unless he went to close the deal, Jason would suspect something was wrong. Hunter notified the FBI, drove to the airport and caught a plane knowing there would be two agents tailing him. He hailed a cab at the airport in New York and was driven to the local docks. There he was shot in the head by one of Jason's men and thrown into the bay. When questioned, the real estate people told the FBI that Hunter never showed up at the office for his appointment. The cab driver, who was paid by Jason, had ducked the FBI tail and said he dropped Hunter out at a bar near the airport. Jason was at the theatre with his family when it all took place, over nine hundred miles away. The next week Hunter's son received a package at his house with more than enough money to get him through school and start a good life.

With Lenny being arrested and held without bond, Jason lost all interest in the business. He was a con man, not a drug dealer and had only gotten involved in the beginning because it was a favor to Lenny. The business was soon handed down to a trusted friend of Jason's. Jason would no longer be involved except as an advisor. He spent thousands of dollars on lawyers, trying to help Lenny. When the trial date came, Lenny testified that Jason simply loaned him money and knew nothing of the drug business. The district attorney knew better but, without Jack Hunter, he had no proof. In April of Nineteen Fifty-Eight, Lenny was sentenced to thirty years in prison. Jason was so hurt by the severity of Lenny's sentence, the betrayal of his trusted friend Jack Hunter and the helplessness he felt that he simply disappeared for three weeks.

The saddest part about betrayal is that it never comes from your enemies.

Anonymous

THE GAME

PART II

10

A prison wall was round us both,

Two outcast men we were

The world had thrust us from its heart.

Oscar Wilde

November Nineteen Fifty-Four. As Jason and Tommy were headed for Orlando, Florida, Jason's mind traveled back through time. His parents were both gone, two marriages, two daughters and a son, so much more than his simple life as a con man. No matter what, the cons and the road pulled at him like a drug. There was so much of his life he just wanted to forget. He worried constantly about Lenny. Jason always enjoyed playing the cons, but somewhere the games had turned into drug wars and murder. Lenny had been in prison six months with what seemed like a lifetime to go. Yet in the midst of this entire nightmare, God had blessed Jason with a son. Jason just wanted to go home and be with his son and family.

Suddenly state patrol cars came from all directions. Jason was told that a warrant had been placed against him for the contract murder of Jack Hunter. He wondered, "All of this happened months ago and I was cleared. What could have happened?" Jason refused to speak and was locked up in the local jail until the Atlanta Sheriff's Department could drive down to pick him up. Tommy was cleared of any charges so Jason told him to take the car to his house and hold it until he called.

When Jason was transferred back to Atlanta, Cheryl came as soon as he called. She vowed to see him through this and put their past behind them. The next day she brought a new wedding band to the jail and placed it on his finger to reunite their love. Jason didn't worry anymore about the charges; he realized how much Cheryl loved him and knew somehow they'd get through this.

Jason was soon taken to court where a surprise witness testified that while she and Jason had been intimate one night, he told her in detail of Jack Hunter's murder and actually admitted that he had done it. The witness was Jason's old girlfriend, Linda Brown. She fabricated her entire story with the help of a district attorney. Linda had been arrested and was being prosecuted for selling drugs, and she had been promised a lighter sentence in exchange for information about any other criminal activity she had knowledge of. She had played some con games with Jason but after she stole five thousand dollars from him, he spread the word among the other local con artists so Linda could not get anyone to work with her. She hated Jason for this so when the police questioned her about criminal activity she offered Jason's name and invented the false testimony with the district attorney's assistance.

Unfortunately for Jason, the jury believed Linda's testimony and convicted Jason. On December eleventh, Nineteen Fifty-Four, Jason Alan Keeble was convicted of conspiracy to commit murder.

All Jason knew about jails and prisons was what he had seen in films or heard from his father. He had been in the county jail now for over a month. He wanted the wheels of justice to start spinning so he could get to a prison and get this over with. Cheryl visited him every Sunday, spending most of her visit crying.

Jason got along well with the other inmates; he was considerate and full of tales of laughter. Most of the men had never had much in life and loved his elaborate tales of the past. One guy Jason met in jail came to him one day saying, "I've got to see that judge today and you've got to cut my hair short so he won't think I'm a hippie." "Cut your hair." Jason laughed, "I can barely cut my nails." Jason ended up cutting the guy's hair with a razor blade and comb. They both laughed at it. Little did Jason know that this haircut would be the first of hundreds of haircuts he would give while in prison.

Nobody in the jail cell had much of anything. Jason always shared what extras he had. The sheriff said they could have a television if somebody got one sent in and Jason was quick to have one brought up to the jail. He had girlfriends visit all the time, willing to bring anything, so along with the TV, he had one of the girls slip a little cocaine past the guard. With a little charm, the guard let her in without even looking in the bag she had.

The television was a great thing to pass the time and everyone in the cell voted on what they wanted to watch. The cell Jason was in was one large cell with room for ten men. There was a shower and a toilet, allowing no privacy at all. One guy in the cell seemed a little strange and one day he asked Jason to let him watch this religious show on television. Jason explained that the TV worked on votes from everybody and the religious show was voted out. At six-fifteen that next morning as Jason slept on the top bunk, the crazy nut had a flashback and rolled Jason off the six-foot-high bunk and onto the cement floor. With one loud sound, Jason had a busted head, a broken hand, a dislocated foot and a broken knee. The nut proceeded to try to kill Jason until another guy in the cell pulled him off. Jason's first thought was to put the nut's name in his private papers and have someone kill him once he was free.

As Jason sat on his bed he thought, "By the time I get out I will have long forgotten that idiot. I don't have bodyguards in here. It's time I take care of myself a little." The nut was now sitting on his bunk reading the Bible as though nothing had happened. Jason took a large drinking cup and limped to the sink. The sheriff had turned the hot water up really hot in an attempt to stop inmates from making fire bombs from toilet paper to heat water for making coffee. Jason let the water run a while and as it did, he took the handle out of the toilet brush and put it in the front of his pants. He then filled the cup with scalding hot water and started to hobble toward his bed. As he passed the nut, he noticed that he never looked up. Jason hit him squarely in the face with the hot water. As the guy came off the bed, Jason began to pound on his head and face with the stick. The guy soon fell and Jason proceeded to pound his hand with the stick until the bones came through his skin, then he beat his face until it was a bloody mess. Jason told him, "Ok punk, get on the bars and make the police get you out of here." The guy ran for the door and screamed until the jailer came back to the cell demanding to know what the problem was. Jason spoke up and said, "The problem is, you put this fucking nut in here with us and he almost killed me. Now get him out." The jailer replied, "We plan to move him by lunch today and I won't tolerate any trouble in here until then." Jason had been almost killed in his sleep and now this jailer wanted to tell him to be a good boy. He slid from his bed, broke the stick and said, "I bet you I can make you move the idiot." With that, he began to stab the guy with the broken stick. The guy screamed in pain and the Jailer opened the door and jerked him outside. It was Jason's first chance to see how the system was run.

On the fifteenth day of January, Nineteen Fifty-Five, Jason was awakened from his sleep and told that the chain (a prison bus) would pick him up soon and to pack his things. He said goodbye to the guys, was cuffed and hauled away.

The first stop was the state diagnostic center in South Georgia. He was placed in a one-man cell. The first thing they wanted was his seventy-five dollar Dingo boots he'd just bought. He knew that a simple plea would never work, so he told the guards about a serious foot problem he had and how he could not walk without the specially made boots. Three days later, he saw a doctor and along with his boot story, he told the doctor of another problem he suffered from, claustrophobia. The doctor was very understanding and gave him a written permit for the boots and arranged for him to live in the dorm. That would get him out of the one-man cell he'd been in. The doctor also x-rayed Jason's bruises from the fight back in the county jail. Although Jason was glad to get the problems looked at, little did he know that it would be the cause of another drastic change in his life.

Cecil and his wife drove to a chain-gang camp in the county where they lived and spoke with the warden about Jason being moved there. After Cecil slipped a few dollars to the guy, the deal was made for Jason to do his time there.

After many tests from the prison doctors, Jason was asked to work in the prison library during the six to eight weeks he had to stay at the diagnostic center. He became the helper of an old con who ran the library. From the library, the con taught him how to smuggle books of pornography back to the men in the cells and trade them for candy and things from the prison commissary. The con told him, "The only thing you have to do is trick the police in the hallway." Jason loved using his conning abilities. He put the books in a place on the bottom of the cart where the fat cop would have to bend over to find them. As he approached the cop, Jason acted new and dumb, asking, "Do you need to search this cart sir?" The cop took one look and replied, "Get on up the hall." Jason made lots of money from that little game which came in the form of junk food and stamps. He shared all he made with the old con who taught him a lot about doing time.

Georgia Prison

Soon a letter came from Cecil and Lynn containing news that Jason would be moved to a small prison camp in Newnan, Georgia and it was very welcome news. Being close to home would allow Jason to see his family more often. On Tuesday morning the rain was falling heavily and the police called the names and numbers of the prisoners who would be transferred that day. Jason had only been there five weeks and expected to stay eight, so he didn't pay much attention until the police said, "Number sixty-seven, Keeble, bag and baggage." He was surprised but very pleased to be leaving that place. He once again said good-bye to his new friends and was chained up to ride. Then the surprise came. He was led outside to a large bus that was painted an ugly green. The bus was marked, "GEORGIA STATE PRISON, REIDSVILLE GA." Jason knew that Reidsville was a very tough prison that was two hundred miles from his home. "There must be some mistake," he told the guards. But the guard just looked at him and replied, "If you don't get on that bus, there

100

will be a real big mistake boy, so get your ass on the bus." With a little kick in the ass, Jason boarded the famous "Green Hornet." Later the prison doctor told him he was at Georgia State Prison because of a medical hold from the injury in the county jail. Now he really wished he'd killed the nut who caused all this. He later found out they used the medical hold to get him there because they needed more white boys to even out the black and white population.

Jason had heard stories about Reidsville and during the two hundred and fifty-mile bus trip, he had plenty of time to dream up the very worst about his next station in life. Finally, the bus stopped in front of the giant prison. As Jason stepped off the bus, he took a long look at the building and thought how big and cold it looked. It was a large white building that looked bigger than the White House in Washington, D.C. It had steel bars and wire fences surrounding the entire place. Not a place he wanted to call home.

Once inside, he was rushed around through clothing issue and to his temporary living quarters. Within two hours he was escorted to classification. There he met another prisoner named L.C. Quick. Quick was very young and flashy with tattoos all over him. He spoke to Jason saying, "You've never been in prison before, have you?" "No," Jason replied. "Well," Quick said, "don't worry, I'll show you the ropes." When Jason finally went before the classification board, little did he know that Quick had already told them, "The guy outside, Keeble, he's with me and we ran together in the streets so whatever you do with me will be fine for him." The administration hated Quick and always gave him the toughest jobs they could. He and Jason were put in Dorm B-Two and the work detail was one that Jason would never forget.

Once inside the dorm, Jason was shocked again. The dorm held sixty men, the windows were knocked out and the outside air blew through them freely. The place was nasty and cold. Quick's friends welcomed them and beds were quickly placed in the corner and there they were, new members of a powerful white click. "Click" was the name used to describe the prison gangs. That evening when the other inmates came in from the work details, Jason studied them all closely. One guy next to him fell on his bed and soon from the shower emerged what appeared to be a female dressed in a bra, panties and a skimpy gown. It was a young "sissy" and after the sissy fixed coffee for his "daddy" and himself, he laid on the bed with his lover while they talked, kissed and stroked each other. For a minute Jason thought, "I might not be able to handle all this."

The next day at five-thirty a.m., the guard yelled, "B-Two Dorm going out." That was work call. Sixty men fell out to an old school bus and were driven to a field near the prison. The guards carried shotguns with long barrels and kept a good eye on all the men. That next ten hours were spent digging up tree stumps. Two men were assigned to each stump and, using picks and shovels, they would literally dig the stump out of the ground. It took about three days to get one out of the ground. At the end of the day Jason went to his bed, laid across it, and the next thing he heard was the hall guard yelling, "B-Two going out." It was the next morning.

The food in the mess hall was terrible and there would be a serious fight in the chow-hall two or three times every week. Everywhere he went, there was a loaded shotgun pointed at him, even while he slept. When the fights broke out in the chow-hall, the guard would fire his gun into the crowd and Jason had to hide behind a table.

The next week Jason thought he might die from the workload. The detail boss took them to a place where the prison raised chickens. The chickens stayed there for twelve weeks before they were slaughtered for use in the prison kitchen. When the chickens were gone, they left quite a mess and it was a job for the inmates to clean up. They would fill up hundred pound sacks and carry them out into the field near the chicken houses. After about three hours of that, Jason was ready to fall out. He told the guard, "Captain. I think I'm going to collapse." The guard was the first black man to ever work there as a prison guard and he wanted to make a name for himself so he played the tough roll. He told Jason, "Go ahead and faint boy, I've always wanted to kill a honky."

This was certainly going to take its toll on Jason and he knew he'd have to get tough with it or die.

Two days before Jason got his first visit from his family, he had a fight with a gay guy who tried to take his wristwatch. The guy ended up in the hospital and Jason had a black eye. Cheryl cried the entire visit. Jason told her, "Don't worry, this guy Quick has been showing me the ropes so I'll be okay."

Jason soon found out he could get most anything he wanted from the other inmates but they wanted cash money in case they ever got a chance to escape. Cash was strictly forbidden in the prison so he asked Cheryl to bring some cash to the visiting room and he slipped it into his boot when the guard turned his head. When the visit was over, Jason always had to strip down his clothes until the guard was completely satisfied that he hadn't tried to smuggle anything in. When the guard checked Jason's boots, the money was sticking out from under the lining of his shoe so they took him to the security office and on to "the hole" -- solitary confinement. The next day Jason was taken to the prison court where he was sentenced to fourteen days in the hole with no mail or visits.

The hole was only seven feet long and four feet wide. It had no lights. There was no bed. Jason was stripped naked and given a blanket to lie on the floor. The cell was so dark he couldn't even see his hands in front of him. The toilet was in the corner. It was a small round hole in the floor. It took Jason two days to find it and he wasn't sure what it was for but he decided to make it the toilet. The trick to that was to use it every third day and beg the guard to flush it every day because the flush valve was outside the cell. Even worse than the stench from the sewer were the rats that would come into the cell from the sewer. Jason had to sit on the hole to block them or risk waking up with them chewing on his flesh. When the guard did flush the thing, the rats and roaches would crawl up into the cell and run around smelling like sewage and who knows what else. In the darkness, Jason never knew when a big rat was in the cell with him, so that kept him awake at night. Sometimes a newspaper would be slid under the door into the cell. Jason didn't know who put it there but it was nice to cover up with on the cold nights. Then one night, as he tried to sleep, a guard shined a flashlight on him and then opened a large fire hose on him and his newspaper. Jason cussed the guard and told him his mother was a bitch whore. One hour later Jason had almost forgotten about it when the guards brought him a real surprise. They opened the door and the light almost blinded him. Then he realized that four guards were inside his cell. The next thing he felt was mace hitting him in the face. They took turns beating him with their nightsticks and kicking him until he passed out and the next thing he knew was when he woke up it was dark and cold again. He could feel the blood pouring from his head but he wasn't sure how badly he had been beaten. For that little incident, he was sentenced to thirty more days in the hole. By this time he had lost ten pounds due to the fact that they only fed him one piece of cornbread and a cup of water each day, and then on each third day they added some partially cooked beans to his tray.

Fourteen days in that hole would confuse the mind, not to speak of what forty-four days did. Jason lost a total of thirty pounds and looked terrible. His only hope was knowing that Cecil had made a deal for him to go to the chain gang camp near his home. When he finally got his mail, Cheryl told him that she had talked to Cecil and that he had a lawyer working on getting him transferred. That couldn't happen soon enough for him.

Time passed slowly with Jason seeing death, homosexuality, gambling and learning many of the games that convicts play. His old pal, L.C. Quick, was making a real convict out of Jason. Then came the summer and the temperature rose to a blistering one hundred and two degrees. Although Jason had told his friend Quick he'd never see the summer heat and the long bean fields, he found himself on a bus and headed to the field. When he stepped off the bus, he took one look at the field and to his surprise, the rows of beans were so long he could not see where they ended.

The guard paired all the men up because of racial tension and then said, "Listen up. Here's how it works. One man will start at the beginning of the row and the other will drop down the row about twenty yards, make a mark there with your foot and start picking. No talking to anyone and no sitting on your ass. These rows take exactly one day to pick and the last pair of men to finish their assigned row will go to the hole." The thought of that hole was still in Jason's mind so he brought it to the attention of the guard that someone had to be last. The guard laughed and replied, "That's right boy, so don't let it be you."

By mid-morning, the temperature was a humid one hundred degrees and with no breeze; it was almost unbearable. Down in South Georgia, they have gnats and deer flies who are like kamikaze pilots. They attack you and don't make any attempt to fly away when you swat them. The gnats flew in Jason's eyes, ears and nose. He scratched so much that he soon drew blood. The guard noticed him scratching and said, "Hey you, boy, you're out here to pick beans so quit digging in your ass and get to work." Jason soon asked an old con how in the hell he kept the gnats out of his face and the old man replied, "Just ignore them and they'll soon go away." Then the deer flies came and they would land on Jason, start biting him and just sit there biting until he killed them.

Soon the guard yelled out, "Gimme a line." That meant the men were to pair off in two lines so the guard could count them. After the count, the guard yelled, "Okay. Ten minutes break."

Jason was about to fall out from the heat and for once he liked what the guard was saying. Just as he was about to sit down he heard Quick yell from the back of the crowd, "Give the break to your mammy." The guard was not able to see exactly who said it so he just waited until everyone had sat down and he yelled out, "Put it back to work." Jason eased over to Quick and said, "Quick you dog, I needed that break." Quick put his little flashy grin on and replied, "Hey pal, don't take nothing from them stinking sons of bitches. Just hard rock it on out."

When the sun seemed its hottest, the guard yelled again, "Gimme a line." This time it was for lunch and Jason welcomed it. Each man was given a brown paper sack with two sandwiches in it. One sandwich had some unrecognizable kind of sliced meat in it and the other was a peanut butter and grape jelly sandwich. The problem was that each time you tried to take a bite, the gnats would cover the sandwich. After watching the other guys, Jason learned to open the meat sandwich, lay one half of it on each side of him and as the gnats attacked it, he would gulp down the peanut butter sandwich. When the day was over and the men were on the bus, Quick asked Jason how it went for him and Jason replied sarcastically, "You're a real pal to get me on this detail with you Quick." Quick and the other guys all laughed out loud but Jason didn't laugh, he was thinking about killing Quick. Jason did notice that none of the men were sent to the hole, so he quickly realized that it had been an empty threat by the guard for the sake of intimidating the men into working faster.

The next morning it all started over again. Guys were passing out, three or four a day, from the heat. Within one week Jason saw men start to cut themselves with razor blades and knives to get out of work details. Men would go to the prison gym and drop weights on their legs and feet. That would get them off work for days. Some would even cut their hamstring which would make them lame for life. With life sentences, what did they care?

Jason couldn't believe the physical condition of some of the guys that were made to work in the fields. When he thought he had seen it all, a strange young man showed up for work. The guy didn't talk much but then he would suddenly yell out at the top of his voice. He would completely stop working and just stare at the sky. The guard yelled at the guy but he just ignored him. For that minor infraction, the guy was locked in the hole for fourteen days. He was then put back on detail, only to end up in the hole again. The guy lived in the dorm with Jason and once when he was released from the hole he found a bed near the corner and put up a giant poster of Superman on the wall over his bed. He never told anyone where he got it. From that day on he was known as "Superman" and every time he heard the name he would smile as if he believed he was in fact really Superman. After a long day in the fields, Superman would never shower or change clothes and he would pace the floors all night. It worried Jason when he would wake up late at night and find Superman pacing the floor. Jason soon learned that Superman was from Forest Park, Georgia, a suburb of Atlanta. Jason also found out that Superman had killed his own mother and went completely crazy. The doctors testified at the trial that he was incompetent but the good judicial system gave him a life sentence for murder and sent him to the state prison as opposed to an institution for the mentally insane.

That next Sunday, Cheryl and the kids visited and Jason looked terrible. Cheryl cried as she watched Jason play with his son and step-daughters. During the visit, Jason mentioned Superman to Cheryl and she remembered him well. They had attended the same high school. She told Jason that he was a very sane man then. He was also a star football quarterback. "Well, not anymore," Jason told her. The visit lasted two hours. That was all the time the prison allowed for visits. The prison staff didn't care that Cheryl had to travel over two hundred miles to the prison from her home. When she and the kids left, Jason cried for the first time since he was a little boy.

Jason soon made friends with Superman and was able to coax him into taking a shower. It was tough talking to him without that bath. As they got to know each other better, Jason found out that Superman had a great talent for singing. Jason felt sorry for him and the many others like him there but he could only do so much to help him.

Jason soon found himself involved in gang wars and single fights. When there was tension between the blacks and whites, Jason and Quick would sleep in shifts to ensure neither would be stabbed to death in their sleep. Then suddenly Jason was transferred to a different unit where he had a private cell. That seemed like a new life. Finally, he could sleep and not worry about being stabbed to death. However, work and the stress were certainly taking their toll on Jason and he thought it would never end.

Three months later Jason was called to the front and told he would be transferred to another prison the next morning. This was the prayer he was waiting for. The small town road camps were much easier than Reidsville and he would be close to his family and all would be well. As he visited with a few friends to say goodbye, a gay guy asked him for his bathroom supplies which were hard to get there. When Jason told him no, the guy hit him in the eye and pulled a knife on him. Jason tried to throw the guy off the third tier but couldn't get past the knife. A friend of Jason's came out and pushed the guy into his cell and locked the door. Jason didn't like to have someone fighting his battles for him and he wanted the satisfaction of throwing the guy off the tier himself but his friend told him, "Hey pal, the sissy just wants you to fuck up and have to stay here in this hell hole with the rest of us. Forget him and get out of here."

The next morning at three a.m. Jason had not slept a wink. Partly because of the anticipation of leaving that place and partly because of stewing over what the gay guy had done to him and how he would get even with him. He managed to buy a glass pint bottle of gasoline from another inmate who worked in the industrial plant at the prison. Suddenly the guard yelled Jason's name. As Jason passed the gay guy's cell, he pulled the glass bottle of gasoline out of his bag and tossed it onto the gay guy's cell floor where it shattered and sent gasoline flying all over the cell floor. Jason was getting ready to throw a lit match when two guards rushed in to see what the noise was. The sissy was locked inside his cell. Jason told the guard, "It's okay captain, I just dropped a shampoo bottle." The sissy was staring through the bars and very glad the guards came. Jason made one last stop to say goodbye to Superman, who just smiled like he did the first time they had met. Jason knew Superman would probably never see the streets again.

One month later, Jason learned that the sissy was found dead in his cell. It seemed that someone forced a pork chop bone down the sissy's throat and choked him to death.

Jason was transferred from the Georgia state prison and never looked back as the bus drove him away. An old man had told him, "Don't look back or you'll be back." Jason believed it. By noon that day he was at a chain gang camp in Newnan, Georgia. It was a new building and very nice. Nothing like the state prison. Newnan was home for Jason and he felt good being there.

Cheryl and the kids were only forty miles away now and visited regularly for the next few weeks. The prison had a barber chair but no barber so Jason told the guys, "I cut hair at the state prison and if you're fool enough to get in the chair, then I'm fool enough to cut your hair." They flocked to the chair and paid Jason one dollar each. Jason did have a natural talent for cutting hair but he was just happy to be able to help someone.

Jason was assigned to a detail that was run by a guard he knew from the streets and his work was made very easy. His job was never the same from day to day. In the summer he'd cut grass on county roads and in the winter he'd run a bulldozer at the county landfill.

Soon Jason could think clearly and he realized that the guys he was in prison with could have money and he wanted some of it. He worked some in the hobby shop but soon decided he wanted to make more money so he opened a pawn shop. The guys all had personal items and he would loan them money on the stuff and charge interest by the week.

He soon met an inmate, named Donny, who had no family to visit him or send him money. Jason decided to help Donny make some money for the both of them. Jason arranged for a girl on the outside to visit Donny and smuggle in marijuana to him during their visits. Donny sold it to other prisoners, who would pawn their belongings with Jason for money to buy Donny's marijuana. Not only was Jason making money off the pawns, he was also receiving half the profits from the sales of Donny's marijuana. He wondered to himself, "Is it the money, or is it the power I have?"

Eight months passed, then one morning Jason was stopped on the way out to work and the guard said, "Keeble, what size pants do you wear?" Jason laughed at the thought of getting new pants and replied, "I wear a thirty-four, why?" The guard told him, "Because the FBI will be here at nine o'clock to pick you up. It looks like you've pissed off the big boys and they want you." Jason left all his things with his new partner and the feds hauled him away.

People don't usually regret doing something, they just regret getting caught.

Anonymous

April is in my mistress' face,

And July in her eyes hath place;

Within her bosom is September,

But in her heart, a cold December.

Thomas Morley

11

The next four months of Jason's life were spent in the custody of the federal government. He was transferred from county jail to court hearings everywhere. He was told that the charge was now for federal racketeering. The U.S. Attorney had gathered lots of witnesses concerning Jason's involvement in the drug wars he and Lenny had gone through.

Lenny was soon brought from the prison where he was being held and put into a cell with Jason. They had a great reunion, discussing the situation at length.

As the trial progressed, witnesses were brought in to testify about Jason's criminal activities. Nothing really pointed to Jason's involvement. But then the second day of the trial brought a great surprise. The girl, Linda Brown, who had testified in Jason's first trial in state court, showed up with yet another tale the district attorney had put in her head. This time she said that Jason had told her about lots of things he'd done during the drug wars. The federal prosecutor brought to the stand six more witnesses that were in jail and had been promised lighter sentences in return for their testimonies that they had worked for Jason involving criminal activities. Jason's attorney cross-examined them as to Lenny's involvement and they all said they didn't know Lenny.

That next day, Jason called Cecil to come for a visit. He asked Cecil to secretly contact some of the jurors to see if any of them would accept a money bribe to hang the jury and cause a mistrial. Cecil did find a juror, an old man, who felt Jason and Lenny were being framed by the girl and, for twenty-five hundred dollars, a deal was made for the old man to hang the jury. The rest of the case was presented to the jury over the next three days and as the jury left the room, the old juror winked at Jason to signal that it would be all right. The jury stayed out for fifteen hours and ended in a hung jury. The district attorney and the judge came to Jason. The judge said, "Young man, it's very evident to me that you bought one of those jurors. If I could prove that, I'd prosecute you immediately, but at this point, we'll be trying you again and again until we get a conviction."

Jason denied any knowledge of bribes. A new trial date was soon set. The judge and district attorney made offers to Jason and Lenny to plead guilty to the charges, with promises of small sentences, but Jason said absolutely not. Then late one night, while in their cell, Jason had to physically restrain Lenny to keep him from calling a marshal and confessing. Jason told him, "I've known you a long time and I love you but we've fought this thing for two months now and the offers just mean they have a weak case. Now you listen to me and I'll promise you we'll beat this some way. You are just letting all these pressures get to you."

During the next trial, none of the new jurors would accept a bribe from Cecil. The girl's testimony was the biggest problem Jason had. Toward the end of the trial, Jason asked the lawyer how things were going and whether he could ever beat this case. The lawyer replied, "Jason, it looks bad and I'm out of aces." Jason told him, "Get a fifteen-minute recess. I want to talk to you." The lawyer replied, "I'll try but it's awfully late to ask for a recess." When the lawyer made the request, the judge's first answer was no, but when the lawyer assured him that he could produce new evidence, the recess was granted.

Jason and his attorney were led to a small private room and Jason said to the attorney, "I realize that this doesn't look good for Lenny and me but I don't see any sense in both of us being convicted of this. I understand that the law says my past and Miss Brown's past cannot be brought out unless you bring it up. I want you to put her on the stand and bring out the fact that she and I have been involved in lots of illegal schemes and scams together throughout the time we've known each other and also be sure to let the jury know that she and Lenny had a confrontation. She hates Lenny and she would do or say anything to get him more time." The lawyer made notes, then looked up from his legal pad and said to Jason, "That will surely mean a conviction for you. Are you ready for that?" Jason nodded yes. They sat for a while longer discussing details.

When court was back in session, Jason's lawyer called the girl who was testifying against Jason to the stand and asked her, "Miss Brown, how long have you known Mr. Keeble?" "Um, about five years," she replied. Jason's lawyer continued, "And isn't it true that Mr. Keeble is now serving time in the Georgia state prison for conspiracy to commit murder?" That statement brought an eruption of murmurings in the courtroom and the judge banged his gavel to quiet them. Miss Brown had been well warned by the district attorney not to bring up anything about Jason's current incarceration because to do so was illegal and would cause a mistrial, so she was completely stunned.

The lawyer waited until the courtroom was silent and continued, "Miss Brown will you please answer the question?" She looked at the district attorney who nodded that it was okay to answer the question. "Yes sir, he is." The jury all set their eyes on Jason. The lawyer went on to say, "Now, tell us, Miss Brown, can you recall the night Mr. Keeble invited you to his house with the understanding that you'd spend the night there with Lenny Patillo, the co-defendant in this case?" "Yes," she answered again. The lawyer continued, "Isn't it true that your ex-husband showed up at the house that night and after a big argument, Lenny Patillo threw you and your ex-husband out of the house. Isn't that right?" Miss Brown looked at Lenny with sharp eyes and answered, "Yes he did and almost broke my arm doing it." The lawyer then asked the fatal question, "Now, Miss Brown wouldn't you like to get even with Lenny Patillo for hurting you?" Just as the district attorney was about to object, the girl yelled out, "Yes! I hate him and I hope he gets fifty years in prison!" Lenny looked at Jason as if to say, "What in the hell are you doing?" The lawyer went to the jury in his closing statement and told them, "Ladies and gentlemen of the jury, by her own admission Linda Brown was very angry with Lenny Patillo and wanted to get even with him, and further that she's known Jason Keeble for many years. She is, as you all know, in prison now for drug sales. I submit to you that Jason Keeble and Linda Brown may have acted together in all types of crimes. It is also obvious that she is saying all she can against Jason Keeble to make sure he stays in prison a long time. I might also add that she cannot be convicted of any of the crimes mentioned here today because she is testifying for the government. To sum it up, Jason Keeble may well be guilty of the charges brought here today but before you put Lenny Patillo in the penitentiary for twenty-five years on her word, you'd better search your conscience." The judge quickly interrupted him to say, "Ladies and gentlemen of the jury, the defense lawyer does not impose sentences on offenders and you are to disregard that last statement of his." That was fine with the lawyer and Jason since the thought had already been planted. As the lawyer sat down at the table with Jason, he whispered, "I guess you know that you just sent yourself to the penitentiary." The jury was out for only forty-five minutes. Lenny was found innocent but they decided Jason was guilty of federal racketeering.

As soon as the jury made its decision and was dismissed, the judge said, "Mr. Keeble, it seems to be your day for tricks. You obviously tricked my jury with that last little story so I hope you will be able to handle the responsibility for the crimes you and Mr. Patillo are guilty of. Therefore, I place you in the custody of the attorney general for a period of fifteen years."

Lenny was sent back to prison with no charges and Jason was waiting to be sent back to the state prison in Georgia in order to complete his pending sentence. By putting a few dollars in the right hand, the federal sentence soon ran concurrently with Jason's state time and he now had a total of fifteen years with a hope of a parole in five years.

During the two trials, Cheryl had made many promises to visit Jason but she only visited once. She assured Jason that she did not have a lover but was very interested in what he would think if she did. One week later when Jason called her, she asked him for a divorce. Somehow he knew she would do that. She said that the lawyer would prepare the papers and send them to him.

Jenny Lawson was an old girlfriend of Jason's. She had been writing to him in prison and asking to come visit him. He finally decided to let her come for a visit. She came the very next day and was excited to see him. She was upset to see how tired and run down Jason looked. She told him that she had always loved him and would wait for him to get out so they could be together.

When Jason was finally sent back to the chain gang camp in Georgia, Cheryl wrote and said she would come on Saturday for a visit. It was quite a surprise for Jason but he welcomed the time to be with her and his son. He gave most of his time to his son because he dreaded hearing more about the divorce that Cheryl was thinking about. When he did talk to Cheryl she told him she had changed her mind about the divorce and vowed to visit every week so they could try and make the marriage work. That made Jason very happy. But this turned out to be her last visit. When the divorce papers came, Jason signed them but only after Cheryl gave him her word that she would bring his son for a visit every month.

When Jason told Jenny Lawson about the divorce, Jenny started visiting every week. Jason had finally settled back into all his old hustles. Three months passed with no sign of a visit from Cheryl or his son. Cheryl would not answer a single letter from Jason. His daughters lived in a small town nearby with their mother, Anna, and step-father. They visited every other week, which was very good for Jason's spirit. He wrote Cheryl letters of hate, betrayal, and pleas promising money for visits but nothing ever happened.

The time in prison wasn't all that bad. Being in the road camp made the work a lot easier, thanks to his friend who was a guard there. Jenny also made his time better by visiting and caring for him but the sad fact remained that he still loved Cheryl and vowed that he always would.

Soon Jenny realized that Jason was still in love with Cheryl and during a visit, told him that she had met a man who had proposed marriage to her. Jason was sad but encouraged it because he knew there would never be any chance for the two of them being together. Jason had spent a lot of free time with Jenny off and on for a year before he went to jail and she saw many exciting things while being with him. She truly did love him and hoped he would settle down someday. Once Jason had been followed to her house and later that night as they slept, the bedroom was shot to pieces by shotguns. Jason placed the mattress over the two of them and no one was hurt. But the bedroom itself was another story. It was a total loss. Jenny knew they were trying to kill Jason and that made him some kind of bad boy in her eyes. After the shooting, he told her that the shooting was a mistake, but Jenny knew better. Jenny thought long and hard about her future with Jason and decided to marry the new guy who had proposed. A short time later she wrote Jason that she would be getting married but wanted to continue writing to Jason. He felt sure that he had done the right thing for Jenny but knew he would miss the special attention she gave him.

Soon Jason asked another girlfriend who had been writing letters to him to start visiting. One month passed and one day while Jason and the new girl were visiting, Jenny showed up. Her arm was in a cast. The guy she had married turned out to be a nut and had broken her arm. Jason told her to go over to her mother's house and he would take care of the guy. Three days later the guy called Jenny to say that he wouldn't ever bother her again. She later found out that he was calling from his hospital room.

Jenny soon became a regular visitor again but they both knew that Jason still loved Cheryl and missed his son.

Some five months later, Jenny had another proposal of marriage and this time she was sure it would work. Jason gave her his blessings and the marriage did work. She wrote to say how happy she was. She still loved Jason but she knew how he felt and she had to make a home for herself and her kids.

Time passed and Jason began to feel like he was accomplishing nothing. One day as he lay on his bed in thought, he asked his friend Bill, "If I could get one dollar out of everybody in the greater Atlanta area, how much money would I have?" Bill thought Jason was crazy but after thinking it over for a minute, he replied, "That should total about two hundred thousand. Why?" "Well," Jason continued, "I just might have an idea to make us a little extra money."

That next week Jason asked Cecil to run an ad in the *Atlanta* newspaper.

Lonely white male, twenty-seven years old.

In prison with no family. Needs friends.

Write Jason Keeble, C/O State Prison, Newnan, GA

Soon the letters poured in and Jason told Bill, "Listen, you answer half of these letters and we'll run some sad stories for a few bucks. Be sure to ask them if they could send a few stamps." Girls, homosexuals, church people and some that were just inquisitive about prison life, all wrote. Jason and Bill asked for and got plenty of material items. Shoes, radios, watches, rings and all sorts of things they could sell to the other inmates. Mostly Jason wanted the stamps and after a few hundred stamps came in, Jason told Bill, "Ok buddy, here is a form letter, I want you to copy it and send it to addresses from the Atlanta phone book." The form letter simply stated that a person who is in prison and realizes his mistakes would like to offer advice to the families and friends of people who might be involved in crime and headed to prison. He asked for a donation of one dollar and a self-addressed stamped envelope for this information.

The letters were sent out for the next six weeks and the money poured in. As letters came in, Jason sent the return letter out that told horrible stories about being in prison. It was a way to make easy money and it did. The first month netted them almost five hundred dollars in cash.

The scam was just getting a good start when the warden got word of the deal and put a cold stop to it. Either Jason was to stop this mess or be transferred back to the state prison in Reidsville, Georgia.

Jason did stop the game but two weeks later he was transferred to a small road camp in Lagrange, Georgia where he was assigned to the toughest detail they had. He knew many people there that he had done time with in Reidsville and soon his job was changed to an easy one. He could even slip away from the prison and meet his girlfriend who would wait near the prison pretending to be fishing in a nearby creek. Her name was Susan. She had met Jason when he was a regular at a nightclub in Atlanta. She fell in love with him from the start only to find out that he was married and wouldn't ever consider leaving his wife. Jason had suddenly disappeared from her life one day and she decided to find him. She asked about him at the nightclub and was told he was in prison. She found him and began visiting every weekend. She was happy to find that he was no longer married and begged him to marry her but he refused. Deep inside, he was still in love with Cheryl. She didn't care. She promised to visit him every week and Jason was happy with that.

On April twenty-third, a letter was delivered to Jason by the local sheriff. It was a court document telling him to either sign the papers allowing Cheryl and her new husband to adopt his son James or appear in court on May tenth. He read the papers and thought, "She didn't even tell me she was getting married." He became crazed and had to be put in a private cell until Cecil could come down and get him calm again.

Cecil did convince him to get a lawyer and fight the case. Jason agreed only after Cecil promised that if he lost, Cheryl would be handled by his friends, along with her new husband.

Jason was soon moved to the Clayton County Jail where the trial was to take place and his case was prepared by an attorney Cecil knew.

The trial day came; Jason was handcuffed and carried into the courtroom. As he walked down the hallway, he saw Cheryl and his son James sitting on a bench but neither looked at him. James was five now. Jason hadn't seen him in about two years. How he had changed. Jason was so proud to see how much his son looked like him. His attorney had a private meeting with the judge and told him, "Your honor, my client is under a great deal of pressure here today because of his love for his son and has asked that you suppress your final decision on this case until he is back in his jail cell." The judge asked why and was told, "Your honor, Mr. Keeble has assured me that he will try to hurt his ex-wife right in the courtroom if he loses his son and I believe him." The judge assured the lawyer that there would be no violence in his courtroom and told the lawyer that Mr. Keeble better remember that.

The trial began with Cheryl, James and the new husband all sitting across a large table from Jason. Cheryl would make no eye contact with him. Jason was so thrilled to see his son that he almost forgot why he was there. He had instructed his lawyer to attack the fact that Cheryl would never tell a lie. Cheryl's lawyer presented a case that asked for Jason to be impeached as a father. The request was based on the theory that Jason was in prison, a known gangster and a danger to society and his own son. When Jason's attorney asked Cheryl how she knew about his involvement in the crime world, she told a very bold lie and said she had no knowledge of his dealings. Jason stared at her and thought, "So much for the saintly wife I thought I had." The judge asked, "Mrs. Anderson, are you telling the court that you had a new home, cars, an unlimited expense account and you thought your husband earned all this money from a real estate investment?" She replied, "Yes sir I did."

The judge then turned to Jason and asked, "Mr. Keeble, are you in fact the biological father of one James Alan Keeble?" With Jason's answer of yes, he directed his eyes to James. James looked back at him, then at his mother and asked, "Mama, who is that man?" Jason knew then that Cheryl had not even shown the boy a picture of him and he felt like choking her right then. The question for the court was whether or not Jason had attempted to see the boy or pay his child support within the past year. Witnesses were called on Jason's behalf to testify that he had made all types of efforts to see the boy and had sent him money. The two witnesses were Jason's girlfriends, Jenny and Susan, and he could see that Cheryl hated those girls being there.

As the case neared the end, Jason felt he was losing and was ready to explode when the judge asked him, "Mr. Keeble, I want to know your reasons for wanting to stop this adoption." Jason thought, "What type of game could I use here to save my relationship with my son?" Then he decided to himself, "I'll just tell the truth and if it doesn't work, I'll send Cecil word and have her and the new husband killed." Little did he know that Cecil and the guy who had killed Blackie were outside at that moment awaiting the decision. Jason looked at Cheryl and his son sitting there; then he looked at the judge and answered, "First of all, your honor, with all due respect, I don't know where you got your God license but it appears to me that you've got one. I was raised to believe that God blesses two people with a child and He is the only one who has the right to take that child away. I love my son and I've never abused him in any way. Cheryl also has two girls that I've raised since we got married and I'm ashamed to admit I've done more for them than I have for my own two daughters. You will notice that her daughters are not here today and the reason is that they will only say good things about me. I agreed to sign the divorce papers only after a verbal agreement between Cheryl and me that I could see my son anytime but this is the first time I've seen him in two years." Jason then looked at the new husband and continued, "You sit here and tell the court that you love my son and want to be his father but the truth is, you love the good times you have with my ex-wife. You're forgetting that I was married to Cheryl for a long time and the only reason you're here is that she says this is what she wants. You've got a lot of nerve to ask to become my son's father when you walked out on your own wife and daughter to be with Cheryl. My advice to you is to sleep with Cheryl and have your own son because you won't get mine with any peace of mind." Jason's lawyer calmed him down while Cheryl's lawyer made a big scene about Jason's violent nature.

Jason then continued, "Cheryl had nothing to do with any of my criminal past but she has told nothing but lies from the beginning of this trial. I'm here today because my lawyer assures me that Cheryl can never take my son from me. You asked why I want to stop this adoption. I'll tell you this much, if your court and the federal courts take my son away from me then I'm better off in prison." Jason then stood up and looked at the judge who seemed to be very concerned about what he was saying. He then turned, looked at Cheryl and her husband and said to the judge, "If this case is decided against me, I will kill those two people." He was pointing his finger at both of them and they both fell deathly white. Jason's lawyer was trying to put his hand over Jason's mouth but it was too late, the damage was done. The judge seemed to ignore Jason's last statement and said, "I want to make the right decision in this case and to be sure that all the evidence is presented. I will allow the lawyers ten days to bring me any new evidence they might find. Otherwise I will decide this case based on what I now have." As Jason got out of his seat, the judge said to him, "Mr. Keeble, I want you to know that if Mr. and Mrs. Anderson have so much as a fender bender I will come after you." Before Jason was led away from the courthouse by the police, he was allowed a short visit with his lawyer and the girlfriends who had testified for him. As they talked, Jason noticed the police locking Cheryl, her husband and James in a small room. It must have been the threats he made. Cheryl's husband was refusing to be locked inside the room with them. Jason thought he'd scare the guy a little so he spoke up in a loud voice saying, "I hope the fuck he doesn't get locked up in that little room, because I want to kick his ass anyway." Cheryl's husband looked at Jason and walked into the room without another word. Jason laughed and thought, "Cheryl got herself a real punk for a husband."

Once Jason was back at the prison, he refused to work and the guards put him back into solitary confinement. Ten days later Jason's lawyer came to the prison to visit and told him, "Jason, I won't beat around the bush with you. The court has made their decision on the adoption and you won." Jason was glad to get the news but he knew he still had no chance of seeing his son for a long time. The court's decision only stopped Cheryl from changing the boy's name. He'd still have to wait until he was free to be with his son. The guards let him out of solitary with the agreement that he'd go back to work. When he got back to his cell, a shower and hot meal were very welcome.

Soon his state parole date came up and he was paroled to the custody of the federal government. The papers read, "You are being released to the custody of the United States Attorney General as we the state feel you will continue to be of no threat to the American public. This action is effective September First, Nineteen Sixty.

Men make counterfeit money; in many more

cases, money makes counterfeit men.

Sydney J. Harris

12

Jason had asked some friends about the federal prison system and compared to where he had been, it sounded like a resort hotel. When the marshals picked him up he asked them which prison he was going to. The driver replied, "All we're doing is moving you to the Fulton County Jail in Atlanta. I have no idea which prison you'll end up in." Jason had heard nightmares about the Fulton County Jail and what went on there. "What in the hell am I going there for?" he wondered.

When he arrived, they quickly threw him into a drunk tank with at least twenty other prisoners, some public drunks and who knows what else. There were several pay phones in the cell so Jason had a chance to catch up on a lot of calls that he'd missed by not having a phone in the state prison system. He was soon carried to a small cold room where he was stripped of his clothes, sprayed with disinfectant, searched for contraband then sent to the regular cell block. The cell was made for sixteen men but twenty-seven were in it so a lot of guys were sleeping on the floor, some with mattresses and some with just a single blanket. The cell was dirty and crawling with roaches. Everybody looked like they'd just been dragged out of a trash can. The guard gave Jason a blanket but he soon learned that as soon as someone got out he could move up to a mattress and then on to a bed. That floor was almost unbearable but Jason made a phone call to a friend on the outside who delivered money to the family of a guy to buy his spot on a bed. The next Sunday he had a girlfriend visit but the visits were set up so that inmates talked on a phone to their visitor while they were on the opposite side of a large piece of glass.

Eighteen days passed with Jason sleeping only about an hour at a time. His first smile came when the guard called his name to be transferred. He was once again locked in chains and put on a bus. The driver told him he was headed for the federal prison in Alabama. Once there, he could hardly believe how nice it was. The place looked like a college campus with a fence around it but the fence was enough to let you know that it was still a prison.

The entry process consisted of answering a lot of questions, enduring another strip search and being escorted to a cell house to be held until they figured out which building to put him in. He was given a suit of khaki pants from the army's hand-down program that was two sizes too big and a pair of very uncomfortable shoes to match. He'd certainly need a tailor here.

The prison was new and the living quarters were five separate buildings that held one hundred and fifty men each, grouped together according to the severity of their crimes. The buildings were set in a circle joining the factory, recreation center and other administrative buildings. There was a large yard in the center of the circle with huge oak trees and walkways to the various areas. The cell that they put him in was very clean and had a nice bed. He was there by himself so he could finally get a decent night's sleep for the first time in eighteen days. Strange...when he first came to prison he lied to get out of being put into a lonely one-man cell and now, he would gladly pay money for some peace and quiet.

The next morning as he was sleeping very soundly, the guard, or as he soon learned, "the hack" opened his cell door at five a.m. and ask if he wanted coffee, milk or both. Jason thought he had died and gone to heaven. He accepted both although he didn't drink coffee. Breakfast was soon delivered to his cell and it was very much like a breakfast at a diner. Jason thought, "I could get spoiled here." The hacks were all polite and called him Mr. Keeble and why not, he deserved it.

After several days in the holdover cell, Jason was placed in one of the regular housing units. He soon learned that he had been placed in a unit with inmates who had committed violent crimes.

The administration found out that Jason didn't have a high school diploma and informed him he'd have to go to school at night. The next week he started classes. The school was run by females from the "free world" and he hadn't been very close to a woman in a long time so it seemed a little weird to him. He took basic education and typing and didn't mind it at all.

Jason soon ran into a couple of old cellmates from the federal holding jail in Atlanta and they told him how to get his inmate clothes altered to make them actually fit instead of hanging off of him like a sack. He was soon looking better and impressing all the ladies at the school.

One of Jason's new friends worked in the prison business office and was going home soon, so he asked Jason to take over his job. Jason agreed and came over for an interview. There he was greeted by an Italian lady about his same age. She was very petite and beautiful. Her name was Mary. Jason asked his friend, "Who is that lady?" His friend replied, "She'll be your new boss." "Oh no." Jason laughed, "I can't work for her, I'll get in trouble with that fine little thing." The girl was standing outside the door and heard everything he said. She hired him that very same day.

Jason was put in charge of the paperwork in paying all the prison's expenses. The job was easy and the office he worked in was nicer than most he had seen in the streets. All the people who worked there were free people from outside the prison who didn't care one bit to play police, and the inmates there all seemed to be good people he could trust. Every time Mary spoke to Jason, he just stared at her and thought, "Lady, if I was in the streets I'd charm the panties right off of you."

As time passed, Jason and Mary became great friends and shared each other's personal lives in great depth. She checked his prison record and found out he was a gangster and that only made her ask him more questions. He could see that she was very taken with him so he teased her along with her questions. She confessed to him that she and her husband were very incompatible. She had married to get away from home, and he was a good provider. She loved to hear Jason tell stories about things he'd done outside prison and he'd talk all day just to be able to look at her.

One day as they were alone in the office, Mary started asking questions, as usual, asking about the kind of restaurants Jason ate in when he lived in Atlanta. He got brave and said to her, "Look, Mary, I'll just take you to one of my favorite places when I get out." She jumped up and ran out saying, "I can't do that and you're not supposed to talk to me about things like that." He laughed because if there was one thing he knew, it was women, and this one was definitely in lust.

Time passed and Mary could wait no longer to see how far Jason would try to go with her. She went to his office and told him, "Inmate Keeble, I want to see you in that office up front at the end of the hall. There are some things I need to discuss with you about your job." Jason didn't think much of it and replied, "I'll be right up there." When he got to the office he found one of the male employees sitting at a desk fooling around with a calculator and his checkbook. They talked for a minute then Mary came in. She shut the door and said to Jason, "I asked Mr. Lewis to come up as a witness and to make sure no one has anything to say about you and me being alone in here. The reason I want to talk to you is to tell you that you've been saying some things to me in front of the other inmates and I want you to stop it." Jason listened to her and was thinking how silly she was. He stood up to leave with a very unconcerned look on his face and replied, "If that's all you wanted you could have told me in my office. Can I go now?" Mary replied, "I didn't want to tell you in there because I didn't want to embarrass you in front of the other inmates." Jason still showed no sign of emotion, so she continued, "I don't want you to be mad Jason; it's just that I need this job and they will fire me if the wrong one hears you flirting with me." Jason was still standing up and Mary stood beside him wanting to make sure he wasn't mad. To smooth things over, she said with a smile, "My God Jason, you are so tall. I never realized just how tall you are." She stood close to Jason as if she were measuring herself, then sat back down only to jump back up and take off her shoes and said, "Look how little I am without my shoes on." Jason had understood the message the first time she stood up but was afraid to go for it with the other guy sitting at the desk. But a second time...he just couldn't resist. He grabbed her and kissed her passionately. At first, she pulled away then, she fell into his arms. The guy at the desk never looked up from the calculator he was playing with. Luckily for Mary, the guy was a good friend of hers. Mary ran from the room and didn't speak to Jason for the rest of the day.

Drugs were very hard to get at the prison and since there were no gang wars like there were in the state prison, Jason decided to smuggle in a small amount to earn some money. "Or is it just the thrill of doing it?" he wondered. His girlfriend back home would take a lip balm container, clean it out, and then fill it with cocaine. She would seal it with nail glue and bring it to him during a visit. Jason would slip it to another inmate who would push the cocaine-filled lip balm container through a hole in his pocket and down to his rectum where he'd give it one push and it was neatly inside him. Once it was, he could simply walk back to his cell and push it out. It was the safest way of transporting and there was no danger of it busting inside and killing the guy. A lip balm container would hold three grams of coke which was worth about four hundred dollars inside the walls. Since inmates were not allowed to have cash, Jason would sell the coke to his friends and have them call their families and friends and get them to mail money for it to Cecil. Once the money was received they got the coke. A lot of people would try to get the coke, then tell lies about the money being sent to Cecil. Everybody wanted to get high and they'd tell Jason anything to get ahold of some drugs. Jason would sometimes trade coke for things the guys could get for him from the prison commissary which came in handy for him.

Soon Jason learned something that he never dreamed possible. The captain of prison security called him into his office and told him all about his drug operation. He called names of all the people who Jason had sold drugs to. He then showed Jason a personnel file that proved ninety-five percent of the prison population was PC (protective custody). That meant they had previously testified against someone and would be killed if they were in other prisons. Some had false ID and names, and would do anything to remain in a safe place. They had told the captain all about Jason's drug operation. He advised Jason to stop it or end up in the United States Penitentiary at Leavenworth, Kansas, which was a very tough prison to be in. The captain of security wanted to take Jason to an outside court and ask the judge to give him another five years for smuggling but the warden said to give him a warning first. As Jason left the office he thought, "How in the hell did I end up here?"

Jason wasn't stupid; he quit smuggling drugs that day. He did, however, hand the business down to another guy who had a life sentence and didn't care about being caught. In the deal with this guy, Jason still made sure he'd have enough coke for himself and a couple of his friends.

With drugs behind him, Jason was working hard and trying to make parole when Mary approached him and said, "Jason, the warden wants to see you in his office. I hope you are not in any trouble." Jason couldn't imagine what it was all about. Mary continued, "Jason, please don't tell him anything about you and me." Mary had been bringing Jason things he needed, including plenty of home cooked food, and she wasn't really sure what he would tell under pressure. It made Jason furious for her to imply he would snitch. He told her, "Mary, I'll ignore that statement this time but if you ever say anything like that to me again, I'll kick your little ass." Jason had a certain look on his face when he was mad and it was easy for Mary to see that he meant exactly what he said. He walked out of the office and left her with a red face and her mouth wide open.

Jason was worried about the warden, but since he knew he was clean, he knocked on the warden's door. The warden said, "Come in Mr. Keeble and have a seat." Jason replied, "Thank you, sir. Did you want to see me?" "Yes, I do. I've reviewed your file and made some calls about you. It seems that you and I have something in common." Jason paused for a minute then asked, "And what's that warden?" The warden replied, "We both love money and the finer things in life." Jason just sat there staring at him as he continued, "Mr. Keeble, I know you hate a snitch; therefore I feel you won't repeat anything we say. I'm sure you wouldn't want to end up in court for some trumped up drug charge. Would you?" Jason knew exactly what he meant. The warden smiled and continued, "Here's the deal. I've got access to a lot of inmate's names and personal information that are locked up here. You being the master con man I hear you are, you should be able to figure us a scheme to make a bundle of money." Jason couldn't believe what he was hearing and his first thought was that it must be a set up.

He thought for a minute then told the warden, "Sir, I love to play the cons but I don't like to get conned myself. So, before I'd play any games with you I'd have to know it was on the up and up." Jason continued: "I mean you'd have to put yourself in a position so that you'd be just as deep in it as I am." This angered the warden but he was cool and replied, "Mr. Keeble, I'm talking to you about breaking the law and that's plenty enough to get me put in here with you so you'll just have to trust me, as I do you." Jason needed some time to think so he said, "Ok warden, I'll put some thought to it but I really don't know a game that we can play from here with a bunch of guys who have no money." As he started to leave, the warden smiled and said, "You'll think of something, won't you?" Jason walked back down the hall toward his office and thought, "The guy is serious but can he be trusted?" Mary was almost standing on her head waiting for the news. Jason just told her it was one of the recent auditors who'd told the warden how helpful Jason was in the last audit and he wanted to thank him personally.

Time passed with Jason worrying about this thing with the warden and just what he was up to. Then his unit team called him in and told him that they had put in for his parole and it had just been approved for June Seventh, Nineteen Sixty. When Jason asked how this came about, he was told the warden wrote a letter to the parole board and stated that he felt Jason would be ready for parole as soon as possible. "Well." Jason thought, "The warden has done me a big favor, so now I'll do this

his way."

That next day Jason saw the warden during lunch hour and told him, "Ok warden, I'll need a few days to put something together but I'm ready to play now." The warden smiled and replied, "Good." As Jason walked away he turned and said, "Oh yeah, I appreciate the letter you wrote to the parole board." "No problem Mr. Keeble. Just show me how much you appreciate it."

Jason and Mary had gotten more involved than ever now so he would work overtime while everyone else took lunch breaks. By doing so, they could spend some personal time and sneak a few kisses and a little petting. Things were good until a guy who worked in the office suspected what was going on. He got busted for having drugs and told the captain that Jason was having an affair with Mary. The captain snatched Jason off the job and sent him straight to a holding cell while they investigated the charges.

For the next seven days, Jason sat in the holding cell and thought about how Mary would get scared and tell all she knew, and then resign from her job. Little did he know that Mary believed Jason when he told her he would never snitch on her and she denied everything they hit her with.

On the seventh day, Jason was released and told to find a new job. As he was being released, the warden came in, took him to a private room and asked, "What in the hell are you doing? Leave these women alone and get your ass to work on our deal or that parole will be down the drain." Jason replied, "Don't worry warden, in the seven days here I figured out what we'll do." Jason didn't want to do any scam that would hurt a fellow inmate, even if they were mostly all rats, but now he was desperate. Jason asked the warden to pull the records on forty people who had been in prison just one year and had not filed any income tax for the last year prior to their incarceration. He then had the warden bring in blank W-2 forms from the streets. He filed income tax returns on these people with the help of a crooked tax lawyer whom the warden allowed him to visit with. The papers were held until the April tax due date and then filed by the attorney. The warden got post office boxes for the returns to be mailed to. When the checks came in, they were cashed by the attorney who brought the money to the warden. The first round grossed them forty thousand dollars. He and the warden did the same thing three times before the tax season was over. The warden was a very happy man and sent Jason's share of the money to the attorney to be held for Jason until he got out.

Jason had been assigned to work on the recreation crew since he had lost his job in the business office. Once or twice weekly, he was called to the hospital for some bogus reason and Mary was always there. Soon a job came open in the hospital. The girl who worked there was Mary's friend who made sure Jason got the job. Now Mary could visit him every day.

Jason had met an old man, Mr. Kitchens. He was an old con artist and counterfeiter. His hustle was printing fake savings bonds and cashing them. He was considered the very best counterfeiter in the entire South. He and Jason spent hours sharing con game strategies. Jason kept notes on all the games that the old man taught him and later shared them with Cecil during their visits.

All of Jason's girlfriends had decided that once the Feds got a man, he was gone forever. They soon stopped visiting. Now it was just Cecil, Cecil's wife Lynn, and Jason's daughters who visited Jason. He had made a deal with a counselor to call Cheryl at her job, using the prison's toll-free phone. In spite of the terrible court battle he had been through with Cheryl, she would still accept his calls. Their conversations were very dry. She quickly told Jason that James was fine and in very good care. Jason would always ask for pictures or a visit and that's when Cheryl would hang up the phone.

It was soon announced that a new girl had been hired at the hospital and would start work on Monday. She was a tall redhead with extremely long legs, a very short haircut, and a perfect figure. Her name was Karen. Jason told his boss lady, "I'll have her on top of my desk in two weeks." They both laughed and went back to work. His boss lady was having an affair with another inmate who worked in the hospital, and she didn't want the new girl to see what was going on. Jason didn't know it, but she would do all she could to put the two of them together so that the new girl would be sure to keep her mouth shut.

During Karen's second week working at the hospital, Jason was in the dental clinic with her. He told her that she was the hottest girl working there and how he would have loved to have known her when he was a free man. Karen, like a lot of the prison employees, was unhappy at home and she welcomed all of his flattery.

From that day on Karen made sure she wore something attractive to work and soon started to bring Jason some special food from her house. The only thing he had to do was make sure that Mary didn't find out about him flirting with Karen. Soon, however, Karen found out that Jason had been involved with Mary. Karen asked Jason to stop seeing Mary and let it be just the two of them. Jason agreed and soon started working overtime so he could be alone with Karen at the hospital. They would lock the front door and make love on the hospital beds as if they were both free and she loved more than anything how wrong it was. Soon Karen found herself falling deeply in love with Jason.

Jason's boss lady was now very involved with the other guy who was working there and soon started bringing in drugs and liquor which the guy was selling to his friends. No one knew it but the captain of security had his eye on her, just waiting to catch her making a mistake.

It was September and word had come to Jason that he would be going to a halfway house in December. The halfway house was a place where inmates would live while in a transitional period back to freedom. He and Mary had made big plans to be together once he was free but Karen was working hard to make sure it was her he would want instead.

Then Mary became pregnant and everybody thought it was Jason's. Jason got word of the pregnancy and decided to quit his job to make sure nothing happened to interfere with his parole. He signed up to become the prison barber. The barber shop was far away from any females and he felt safe there. He was pretty good at cutting hair and surely he could stay out of trouble there.

Then suddenly in October Jason was arrested by the guards and charged with attempting to enter narcotics into the institution and was placed in solitary confinement. The guards knew that the drugs were not Jason's but hoped to squeeze him into telling on the inmate that Jason had previously given the drug business to at the prison.

Karen had been bringing some designer sunglasses into the prison while Jason was still working with her. Jason was selling them to the other inmates. When Jason had quit his job and gone to work in the barber shop, Karen locked the glasses in the trunk of her car. Then one day, the tail light on her car went out, and without asking, her husband took her keys and opened the trunk to replace the bulb. He found the sunglasses and confronted Karen about them. She admitted to her husband what she had been doing to help Jason. Her husband was livid to think that Karen had been involved in any such mess and told her to either turn the glasses into security at the prison or he would do it himself. Karen told security what she had done bringing glasses into the prison for Jason. She admitted that she knew the glasses were illegal but figured they couldn't hurt anything. Jason denied any knowledge of the glasses but was soon taken before the prison IDC (institution disciplinary committee) and charged with attempting to bribe a staff member, which was a serious charge. He knew there was no attempt to bribe, yet Karen had written the report after security told her she could save her job by doing so. She was fired three days later. Jason was found guilty and given ninety days in solitary, sixty days were added to his time and the decision was made to transfer him to another prison. This killed his chance of being set free in December.

One day as Jason sat in solitary, the warden came by and said to him, "Hey guy, I'd like to help you but there are too many eyes on this. Your dick is going to be the death of you so take my advice, leave it in your pants and stick to the cons. You are very good at that." As the warden turned to leave, he turned and added, "Oh yeah, you not telling them about our deal proves to me that you are a real man. Thank you."

After his ninety days in solitary were up, security decided to transfer Jason to the U.S. Penitentiary in Terre Haute, Indiana. Once there, he was told that his records showed him to be a very powerful con man and a violent man and that he'd better sit quietly there or he might never see freedom again. They seemed very serious about that.

The old prison in Indiana was built in the twenties and held many sad stories. Jason soon met all the old cons that had been there most of their lives who told him many of their stories.

In June of Nineteen Sixty-One, Jason received a notice that his parole date had been changed to August. Thank God. Maybe this would be over soon but he had many decisions to make about where he would live. His youngest daughter, now fourteen, was planning on living with him and that made him very happy. He had to find a good place for them to live together but how would he do at raising a fourteen year old girl? Then there would be getting to know his son who was now nine years old. He called an old girlfriend, Donna, who now lived in Atlanta and she invited him and his daughter to live with her. He thought, "This will be a good place for me to start over."

Karen from the prison had taken another job but still lived with her husband who had caused Jason's delay in being free. One night as Karen and her husband were leaving a local restaurant, they were robbed and her husband was beaten almost to death. The Feds questioned Jason about it but he told them to call his lawyer and get the hell out of his face. What could he do from prison? He soon learned that when her husband was well, they moved without telling anyone where they were.

August sixth came and with no air conditioning at the prison, Jason was ready to leave. He chose to take a bus home so he'd have a chance to spend some time getting back in touch with the world. On the bus trip, he met a young lady whose car had blown an engine and stranded her. She had decided to take the bus home. Jason started a conversation with her and soon explained that he'd just gotten out of prison after five years. Her first question was "How long has it been since you've had sex?" When he told her five years, she smiled and said,

"I'm going to the restroom, give me five minutes and come on back. If you dare." Jason smiled and decided that the good life was going to jump right back into his hands.

When he reached the bus station in Atlanta, he was met by his girlfriend, Donna. On the trip to her house, he couldn't stop thinking about the girl on the bus. He had gotten her phone number but he knew he would never call her. There were just too many things he had to catch up on. His first night passed with only a few phone calls to some of his friends, then it was directly to bed for some rest. The bus trip and that little stand-up sex had worn him out.

For to be free is not merely to cast off one's chains, but to live in a way that respects and enhances the freedom of others.

Nelson Mandela

13

Jason's thirty-fourth birthday came. He really didn't know what he wanted to do except stop aging. Prison had made many changes in his life. He was frightened to be near people and always worried about saying the wrong thing. Donna invited him out to a movie that night. It was over around nine and Jason felt it would do him good to get some rest. When they arrived home, the lights came on and sixty people yelled, "Happy birthday Jason and welcome home." Donna had planned a huge party without him knowing anything about it. The only guests Jason recognized were Cecil, Cecil's wife Lynn and Jason's daughters. There must have been at least fifteen single women at the party and they all looked like they had lots of class. Donna said to Jason, "All my girlfriends are here so just pick one and I'll tell you all about her."

The party was nice but everyone soon started asking questions about prison and Jason didn't want to talk about that part of his life for a long time. Soon he felt like a painting on exhibit so he slipped out onto the patio for some fresh air. That was one of his new treats in life now. The night sky was perfectly clear and the stars shined a brilliant white that seemed to light up the night. There were no prison guards yelling at him, "Lockdown. Count time." "It must be true," he thought. "I'm free again. I'm really free." Just then the door opened and a tall blonde came out. Jason didn't know her and thought she must need some fresh air.

She stopped near him and said, "Excuse me, I'm not trying to interrupt your moment with the stars but I'd like to talk to you." Jason asked her to sit down, thinking to himself, "She could only be another one of those people wanting to know about prison." She sensed his thoughts and said, "I could tell you were uncomfortable in there with all the questions but I thought you might like a little company without all the questions. I'm Victoria and I've tried all night to meet you. Donna told me all about you before you came home. I feel as though I already know you. I must tell you that I'm very frightened of prisons so I don't care to talk about that part of your life if that's alright with you." She giggled and Jason knew that it had been obvious how nervous the questions made him. He thought, "Young lady you and I will get along just fine." They talked and enjoyed the fresh air until Donna came out and said, "I've looked all over for you Jason. Here you are hiding with my neighbor. Is everything all right?" Jason replied, "Well, I'm being attacked by this voluptuous blonde but I'll try to wrestle her off." They all laughed and Donna said, "You watch Victoria closely, she's asked me a lot of questions about you ever since I first showed her a picture of you. She's one of those rich lonesome widows."

The party ended and Jason asked Cecil and Lynn to take his daughters home. Jason had other plans for the evening. He spent the rest of that night at Victoria's house and for the first time since he was with the Madame in New Orleans, Jason had to admit that she was more than he could handle.

The next day Donna took Jason to buy new clothes and with the money he had made with the warden from the prison in Alabama, he could spend a bundle on clothes. He asked Donna to pick all the material and had the suits handmade. She picked the finest shirts and ties sold. She also picked shoes to match each suit. He ended up buying ten pairs. This would at least make a good start on his new wardrobe. Since the clothes had to be handmade, he bought some jeans, a pair of boots and some pullover shirts. Donna also picked out three nice outfits for herself, which Jason paid for. Donna had been a good friend to him over the years and he would do anything for her. He was finally starting to feel like he looked decent for an old man.

Jason needed a driver's license, so Donna drove him to Forest Park where the Georgia State Patrol office was. He had studied the driver's manual prior to coming home and passed the test with ease. As they started to leave the license bureau, Jason remembered that Cheryl worked just across the street at a small office. He figured this was as good a time as ever to let her know he was home. He asked Donna, "Would you please pull into that parking lot over there at the building with 'Food Services' written on it? I need to see someone who works there for a minute." Donna agreed and pulled right up to the front of the building. As Jason got out of the car he said, "I won't be long." He walked in and there was an attractive woman at the front desk. She had great legs but Jason didn't have time for flirting; he had business to take care of. "Good morning, young lady." Jason said. "I need to see Cheryl please." The girl looked at him for an extra second and replied, "Just a moment sir." She disappeared down the hall and Jason couldn't help but take another look at her slim body and the great little walk she had. She went into Cheryl's office and announced, "There's a guy here to see you. I didn't get his name, but he's a real hunk."

Soon she came back up front and said, "Cheryl will see you now, Sir. Her office is down the hall to the left." When Jason walked into Cheryl's office, she thought, "I knew who it was and Margo was right, he looks better than ever." Jason broke the silence, "Hello Cheryl. You look surprised. I won't be here long. Do you mind if I sit down?" He sat down before she had a chance to answer. Cheryl started asking all sorts of questions about when he had gotten home and how he was doing. Jason interrupted and said, "I got home this week and you could care less about how I'm doing. I came here because I wanted you to see me in person. This way there will be no mistaking that I'm back. I want to see my son." He then picked up a pad from her desk and wrote his address and the phone number at Donna's. He handed it to her and said, "You name the place where I can visit my son and I don't want you there during the visit. The information you need is on that paper. I want you to get the papers drawn up for my visitation and I'll start the support payments January First, Nineteen Sixty-Three. I'll call you on Monday. I don't remember any of the past now. I want this thing with my son and me to work, and only you can make sure it does." He got up and walked around the desk and said, "I'm home now Cheryl and you only call half the shots so don't underestimate me again. When I call on Monday, have the papers ready or we go to court." As he started to walk out of Cheryl's office she said, "Jason, your son is just down the street from here; would you want to see him now?" "No," he replied, "I'll wait until it's all legal."

As Jason was leaving the building he felt much better and decided he would make sure the secretary knew he thought she was hot. He made eye contact with her and said, "Thank you young lady...and have a nice day." He was, of course, giving her his best smile and all she could utter was, "Goodbye." She went directly to Cheryl's office, where she found Cheryl in tears and asked, "Cheryl, what is wrong? What happened? Who was that guy?" Cheryl picked up a picture from her desk of her son, James, and said, "Look at this picture and see if you see any resemblance to the man who just left." Margo looked at the picture with a puzzled look and then exclaimed, "That's James' father." Through her tears Cheryl replied, "Yes." Margo was trying to calm her down but couldn't help saying, "Cheryl, he's gorgeous." Cheryl smiled and said, "He never smiled at me today. He always smiles." Margo turned to leave the office saying, "Let me know if I can be of any help to you Cheryl."

Margo

That night Cheryl called Margo saying she was near her house and wanted to visit. Margo lived alone, had been married once for six months to a loser and she now dated very little. She was thirty years old and a very beautiful woman. She told Cheryl, "Sure, come on over." They visited a while and Cheryl finally said, "Margo, you asked today if you could help. Well, you can. Jason will not come to my house to get James because he doesn't want to be anywhere near me. Since James doesn't really know his father, I have to find a place for them to meet and get to know each other. I was wondering if you might let them meet here at your house since James knows you so well." Margo thought for a minute and replied, "I can handle that Cheryl. Just say when." Cheryl thanked her and said, "If they could just meet here until James is comfortable with Jason and then he will pick the boy up and take him to his house." Margo agreed and after a long talk about all the mess between her and Jason, Cheryl left. Margo wanted to help Cheryl but even more so she wanted to get to know Jason.

On Monday when Jason called, Cheryl said, "I've worked it out and the papers are drawn up. You'll meet James on Saturday at my friend's house. Her name is Margo Harris. She lives at 1302 Moore Way in Forest

Park. You met her in my front office the day you stopped by to see me. I will leave James there along with the papers for you to sign and I'll be gone by ten a.m..." Jason again made it plain that he did not want to see Cheryl again and to be sure she wasn't there when he arrived.

The following Saturday Jason was both skeptical and nervous about the upcoming visit with his son. He decided to take a friend with him and told the guy to simply say hello and sit quietly as a witness. Jason knocked on the door of a beautiful home and Margo opened the door. He said, "Hello, my name is Jason Keeble and you must be Miss Harris." She smiled and replied, "Yes, I've been expecting you, come right in." Jason introduced his friend and Margo said, "Please have a seat and I'll get James. He's in the back yard playing." To Jason's surprise, his former step-daughter Angie, now twelve, came running in alongside James and that was even better. Jason had missed her as badly as he had James. He gave her a long hug and said, "You look just as beautiful as ever and now you're all grown up." Angie had grown to love Jason very much when they lived together and she was thrilled to see him. Then Jason turned to see James and said, "And you must be Mr. James Alan Keeble." James was bashful and when he did finally speak, he said, "Are you my real daddy like Mama says?" Jason replied, "Yes I am son." And with that, he produced a package and said, "I brought you a present." The box was almost as big as James. When he opened it he found a giant toy race car. All of a sudden there was no room for being bashful. James' face lit up and he was ready to accept anything Jason said. Jason stared at him and couldn't get over how much like himself the boy looked. He wanted to just grab James and cry with joy but he knew better. That could ruin the entire thing. As James played with his new car, Jason sat with Angie in his lap. Margo just stood back and watched. It wasn't hard for her to determine one thing about this cold-hearted gangster. He was really weak with children.

Margo and Angie talked while Jason played with James and his new car. Suddenly the phone rang and Margo said, "Hello, how are you? Hold on just a minute." She laid the phone down and went into the bedroom. Peaking her head out the bedroom door, she asked Angie to hang up the phone. The call was from Cheryl. "Is Jason there, yet?" Cheryl asked. "Yes he is," exclaimed Margo. She blurted out, "He really is a gangster like you said." Cheryl paused and asked, "Why do you say that Margo?" "Because," Margo replied, "he has a bodyguard with him that doesn't ever smile." Cheryl chuckled, "I'm not surprised. When I lived with him he was never alone." Margo continued, "I just can't see someone who is so charming being so tough." Cheryl asked, "How is he doing with James?" "Wonderfully," Margo said. "They hit it off like they'd known each other for years. Jason brought a race car for James and that was all it took. He and Angie also had a lot to talk about so all is well." Cheryl said, "Ok, I'll go. Please don't let on that it was me who called." "Sure," Margo replied. "But if it wasn't for the bodyguard, I might attack Jason." Cheryl laughed and said, "I know what you mean. I'll see you this afternoon when I pick up the kids."

The first visit ended well. When Jason left, James hugged his father's neck and told him that he loved him and loved the truck he got. Jason left money for the kids with Margo. He complemented her on her beautiful home and offered her twenty dollars for the time he was there. Margo didn't want money but Jason insisted and she was a little worried about what Jason's bodyguard might do, so she took it.

For the next month Jason met James and Angie at Margo's and soon they all went out together for ice cream. Jason never brought the bodyguard again for which Margo was grateful. Once during a visit, James and Jason went to the store alone and Jason wanted to just drive away with him and never come back.

On their next visit, Jason invited James and Angie to start spending weekends at his house. Cheryl said it would be okay. She knew that James was really enjoying the time he spent with his father. Suddenly Margo realized that her little visits with Jason were about to come to an end and she wasn't sure if she'd ever see him again. On the day of his last visit with James at her house, Jason sent eleven roses to Margo and when he arrived he gave her the twelfth one. That was one of his old traditions. She couldn't believe it when she read the card.

Later at Margo's house, Jason said to her, "I need a permanent place to pick James up so I'll pay you one hundred dollars per month if you'll be the one who takes care of that." Margo replied, "Jason, I'd be happy to have Cheryl drop your son off here every week. I enjoy seeing him but I won't take your money." Margo called Cheryl and the deal was made. Margo thought, "This way I'll be able to see Jason every week." She was very taken with him but just couldn't tell him and wasn't sure if he even noticed her.

Jason was going to be on parole from prison for a while. He needed a steady job so he and an old friend, Henry, talked and decided to open a small used car lot. The idea was to do their own financing and let people pay weekly payments. They opened the place with thirty cars. Cecil stopped by when he was in town to give Jason a pep talk about living right and to wish him luck. Cecil knew that, no matter what, Jason would soon be tempted to hit the road again to be with his one true love, the con games. Jason told Cecil, "For the present time, the car lot keeps me busy and keeps my parole officer off my back but yes, I do have a few things I want to do." His parole officer was a lady. She was very nice but told him to avoid any type of crime or he would be going back to prison.

A month passed and Margo saw that Jason wasn't going to ask her out so she decided it was time to make her own move. She called him at work and said, "Jason, I was wondering if you'd like to come over to my house for dinner one night this week. I'd like to hear all about how you and James are doing." Jason had decided to leave Margo alone for fear that she might be trying to help Cheryl get him put back in prison but this offer was sure tempting. He had made a connection with her from the moment they met. Jason learned in prison that you trust no one. Some of his old friends thought he acted strangely but each time he had trusted someone, it caused him trouble. Margo had been nothing but honest with him so maybe he could take a chance with her. "Miss Harris," he told her. "I really can't get away until Friday so if that's convenient, I'd love to come over." "That will be perfect. I'll expect you around eight and, by the way, what would you like to eat?" Jason's first thought was issher but he wouldn't go there. He grinned and replied, "It really doesn't matter, just so I have a bottle of good Scotch whiskey and a warm fireplace." They hung up and Jason thought, "She's probably worth a nice gift so I'll get her something special to make sure she remembers me."

The next day while Margo was at work, she told Cheryl of her plans with Jason. "Cheryl, I've invited Jason over for dinner this Friday and I just wanted you to know about it." Cheryl studied her face for a minute and replied, "You're in love, aren't you?" Margo blushed and said, "I don't know, I've never been in love but so far it feels good so I want to see where it goes. I just want your blessings before I do it. If what you say about him is true, I'll get hurt so I'll take it real slow." Cheryl said, "You can't help falling for him. He has that special something with women and believe me, he knows what to do." They both smiled and Margo said, "I just thought you should know about the date." "It's fine with me Margo, don't miss sleeping with him, he's good in bed." Margo's face turned blood red and she almost ran from Cheryl's office.

When Cheryl was alone she thought, "I don't love Jason anymore, do I? Why do I get upset when I know he's with someone and why does it bother me that we don't see each other? Oh well, that's life I guess. I just never really believed he would ever get out of prison."

On Friday night Jason sent eleven roses to Margo's house and a singing telegram to announce his arrival. It thrilled Margo that he was finally showing some interest in her. When he got to her house, he presented her with the twelfth rose. It was taped to a box and when she opened the box, she found a beautiful full-length mink coat. She was so excited and overwhelmed she could not speak. Jason put the coat on her and when she turned around to let him see it, she was so excited that she fell into his arms and kissed him passionately. Then she realized what she had done and she started babbling apologies. "It's ok." Jason said with a big smile, "If I'd known I would get that kind of thank you, I would have bought two coats." Margo suddenly stared out the door and said, "I hope you didn't bring your bodyguard with you this time." Jason sighed and replied, "He's not a bodyguard Miss Harris." Margo smiled and said, "Just the same, I like it better when you're alone and from now on, my name is Margo."

They had drinks and small talk about the kids. They sat down to a fine meal that she had prepared. She never took the coat off while they ate, and hardly touched her meal. She just sat rubbing the coat and watching Jason eat.

They soon settled by the fireplace. Margo turned on some music and sat on the sofa next to Jason. Suddenly she found herself asking him a lot of questions about his life. The topic was nothing but "Jason" until he slid down onto the big rug near the fireplace. Margo hesitated a moment then crawled into his arms. So much for taking it slow. Jason soon decided to find out if he'd be spending the night with her. He said, "Well young lady, I better be on my way before you try something crazy like attacking me." She raised her head and without a word, kissed Jason passionately. That should answer any questions he had. They did spend that night together and although Margo didn't know it, the fact that she slept in the mink coat was very exciting to Jason. He wanted to ask her to keep on her high heels but there would always be another night.

Jason was doing well with the business he had. He was also trying to sleep with every woman he met and it was about to wear him out. He saw Margo on regular nights but never let her know about the other girls. He was spending little or no time with his real daughters. The oldest one was in chorus at school and the younger was involved in drama classes. His young daughter also wanted to come and live with him when he was free from prison, but Jason had a long talk with her and they decided to wait until he was more settled. His son was a miniature Jason and wanted everything he saw.

Jason's need to travel and play the con games was pulling at him more and more now. His parole officer said he could only leave the state if he was buying cars for his business, so he used that as an excuse when he needed to play his games out of town. With Lenny still in prison, Jason needed a new partner to help him with the games, but who could he trust? The only game he could play locally was the necklace game. He really needed a sharp girl to play with him, but who? After some thinking, he decided to ask Margo out to dinner and discuss it with her. She was crazy in love with him and she loved his stories from the past. Maybe she would like to be a part of it.

She would do anything to be with him and she was taken with the excitement of doing something she knew was wrong. That next Friday Jason went to a friend who was in the jewelry business and bought a necklace with three large diamonds mounted on it. He got a written appraisal of the necklace then carried it across town, sold the stones and had them replaced with imitation stones. He also had the guy set the largest stone back in the necklace with glue that was easy to break loose. That would make it easy to push the stone out.

That evening Jason went to the manager of the Coach & Six restaurant on the north side of Atlanta and made reservations for Margo and himself. He used one of his phony names and told the manager that it was his and Margo's anniversary. He then asked if the manager would keep the necklace and bring it to the table that night while they were eating. The manager was hesitant at first, but the fifty dollar bill that Jason gave him was enough to persuade him and the deal was made. That night Jason picked Margo up at her house and he could tell right away that she was very nervous. He told her, "Don't worry, it will be all right. Just do as I told you. Relax and have fun. That's the best part of it. The money means nothing." Margo had great faith in Jason so she put on her new mink coat and away they went like Bonnie and Clyde.

They drove to the restaurant and the manager rolled out the red carpet for Jason as he and Margo were seated at the best table in the house. Once they finished a meal that was fit for a king, the manager acted on a nod from Jason and brought the necklace to the table. He placed it on the table in front of Margo. She was supposed to act very surprised and when she saw the necklace she really did fall in love with it. Jason watched her face and thought, "Don't overdo it, lady." Jason took the necklace and placed it around her neck saying, "Happy Second Anniversary Darling!" Coffee was served and ten minutes later Jason suddenly dropped his cup smashing it all over the floor. As everyone in the restaurant stared, the waiter rushed to his table as he sat there in shock. When he regained his composure, he said loudly, "My God, the stone is gone from your necklace." Margo looked at it and started crying. Restaurant workers started helping Jason and Margo comb the floor area around the table looking for the stone. The manager looked very worried and other customers were annoyed with the confusion. Jason finally stopped searching and told the manager that it was just one of those things. "Surely it will turn up somewhere." He gave the manager a business card and told him, "When you find the stone just call me and I'll pay you two thousand dollars reward." The manager looked relieved and of course wouldn't let Jason pay for the meal.

Cecil was waiting outside for them and asked, "Well kid, how did it go?" Jason replied, "Real smooth. He's all yours now." Margo then handed the stone to Cecil. She had popped the stone out of the necklace and put it in her bra. She and Jason drove home discussing the game. Somehow it really excited Margo.

After a few minutes, Cecil went into the restaurant and sat two tables away from where Jason and Margo said they had sat earlier. During his meal, Cecil dropped his fork and as a few people looked over at him, he bent over to get it and came up with a big shiny diamond. He made sure the waiter was looking at him then he said, "My, my. What a lucky day for me. This looks like a diamond and it's as big as my thumb." He held the stone up to the light and the manager rushed him like the police would do a criminal. They examined the stone together and Cecil said, "This is some stone. It must be worth a thousand dollars." The manager didn't want Cecil to get the smell of money in his nose so he replied, "Sir, that stone was lost here earlier tonight by a good customer of ours. You are on private property and have no rights to this property," Cecil decided to get real loud but the manager cut him off by saying, "Let's go into my office and discuss this matter." Cecil followed him, mumbling something about how he should have just kept his mouth shut and the stone would have been his.

Once inside the office, the manager again explained the situation with the stone and asked Cecil to give it to him. He never once mentioned a reward and that was Cecil's cue that he was being greedy. Cecil looked at the stone for a moment then said, "Look, I'm sure there is some type of reward for a stone this size. I'm from Florida and need to be getting home so either you call the customer while I'm here and share the reward with me or I'll call the cops here and disrupt your business with a lot of loud talk for the rest of the night." The manager squirmed in his seat for a minute and then he replied, "Look, there is a reward for the stone but this guy spends a lot of money here and I don't want to accept money from him. Here's what I'll do. I'll give you five hundred dollars if you'll just give me the stone and leave." Cecil laughed and replied, "That's crazy. The guy who owns this stone would probably pay a lot more than five hundred bucks to get this back. Call him down here." The manager knew if he called the customer that he could lose the reward altogether. He told Cecil, "I cannot ask my customer to pay a reward after he has spent so much money eating here. So, I'm prepared to pay you seven hundred dollars and that's it." Cecil looked him straight in the face and said, "Either you give me a thousand dollars or I'm calling the police." The manager knew he was cornered but he could still make one thousand for himself so he paid Cecil the money from the cash drawer which he planned to replace with the reward money when his customer came to pick up the stone.

Later that night, as Jason, Margo and Cecil were having a drink together back at Margo's house and discussing their little con, the restaurant manager was clutching the fake diamond that Cecil had sold him and dialing the number on Jason's fake business card, which belonged to a payphone.

Jason gave Margo five hundred dollars and offered Cecil the same but Cecil refused to take it saying, "No charge on this one son, I enjoyed seeing you get started again." Jason replied, "You know that I don't care at all for the money so go ahead and take it." Cecil shook his head and as he was walking away, he said, "Take the money and buy the kids something with it." Jason thought for a minute and decided, "I'll do just that."

It was Jason's first real con in a long time and he loved it. He also liked Margo and considered working with her on a full-time basis. He thought, "She might make me a good wife, I'll spend some time with her." But he knew he'd never get over Cheryl.

Jason and his partner from the car lot were doing a great business. They had named the place "Wheels-N-Deals." It was a good place for Jason to meet people and reestablish himself. With almost eight years of his life gone, Jason needed to learn what made the new generation tick.

The new cars were out on the market and Jason bought a brand new Nineteen Sixty-Three Lincoln Continental sedan. The car had a solid white body, which happened to be Jason's favorite color for a car. The interior was also white, with red appointments. A big part of his playboy image was to have a car that was very impressive. To Jason the car became a castle when he was in it. It was as though no one could touch him. He was at the controls of a beautiful machine and he could make it take him anywhere he chose.

His nightlife with the women and cocaine made it tougher all the time for him to get up in the morning. He made a deal with his partner Henry that allowed him to start work around noon and keep the lot open until eight at night. That gave him a few extra hours to sleep in the morning.

Friday was normally a fast day at the car lot, but this particular Friday seemed very slow. Jason had all the paperwork caught up so he decided to close up early so he could go home and rest up for a long night that he was planning. Just as he was about to leave, the phone rang. Jason answered, "Wheels-N-Deals, Jason Keeble speaking." There was a pause, then a female voice said, "Jason, this is Mary from the prison in Alabama. How are you?" Jason was a little surprised but answered, "Fine, and how is my favorite little boss?" She giggled and said, "Jason I want to come see you if I can." Jason asked, "Is there a problem Mary?"

"No." She replied. "I just want to see you." It was the first time Jason had heard from Mary since she'd quit her job at the prison. He said, "Mary, I haven't seen you in months and you want to just run over here? It's one hundred and twenty miles. What's the deal?" Mary replied, "Jason I've just missed you very much and it hurt me when you got mad at me. I called the number you gave me before I left the prison and they gave me your work number. Won't you please see me?" Jason did care for Mary. He finally told her, "Okay Mary, I'll see you but I'll have to get someone to pick you up. When do you want to come over?" "Don't worry about sending a car for me," Mary told him. "I'll drive myself over. I want to come today but I can't get away until about five o'clock. The baby is with my mother and I need to get dressed first." Jason asked, "By the way Mary, was the baby a boy or a girl and what did you name it?" Jason really didn't want to know but he thought he could at least be polite. Mary replied, "I had a beautiful little girl and her name is Christy Ann."

Jason said, "I'm very proud for you Mary. That baby should be mine but that's not important now. If you still want to come over, you take Highway Seventy-Eight to Atlanta. Go south on Stewart Avenue. Take a right at the fifth light and my office is on the left about a quarter of a mile up the street. Just look for the sign that says, "Wheels-N-Deals." Mary replied, "I've got it and I'll be there around seven-thirty tonight." Jason said, "I need to spend some time with my kids so if you don't mind, I'll probably pick them up when you get here. Will that be a problem?" Mary said, "I don't care where we go or who's there, I just want to be with you." "Okay lady," Jason replied. "You be careful and I'll see you tonight." At least this would give Jason a break from his long nights out.

Mary arrived just before seven o'clock. Jason gave her a big hug hello, and introduced her to his partner Henry and his secretary Jeanette, and then he asked Mary to just hang around while he took care of a few things before they left. Mary agreed and took a seat in the reception area. Just then the phone rang and Henry said, "Jason, its Jerry at City Chevrolet down the street." "Ok Henry." Jason answered the phone saying, "Yea Jerry, what's up?" "Hey, Jason." Jerry replied. "I need to sell you that Grand Prix you looked at today." Jason said, "Jerry I'll take the car but the price is still five hundred like I offered you this morning." Mary was seated just outside Jason's door and overheard his conversation. She thought to herself, "He's probably a real good businessman." Jason could also see her face and he was thinking, "You look better than ever and now I don't have to hide from the guards, I'll show you a few tricks." Just then Jerry's voice came over the phone saying, "Jason I need to get eight hundred dollars out of that old car." Jason sighed and replied, "Jerry, You've shopped that car all over town and I'm the highest bidder on it or you wouldn't be calling me so either sell it or hang up your telephone." "Ok Jason." Jerry said. "But you owe me one." Jason hung up the phone and smiled because he really did love arguing over those old cars. Henry asked, "Well, did you buy it?" Jason replied, "Yes I did." Then he turned to his secretary Jeanette and said, "If you'll make me a check for five hundred dollars to City Chevrolet, I'll send the porter down there to get it."

When the porter returned with the car, he parked it out front. Henry came through the front office and said, "Let's take a look at this five hundred dollar cream puff you bought." Jason smiled and said, "Yes sir, boss." He got up from the desk and followed Henry out to the car. On the way out, he gave Mary a little smile and said, "I'll be right back."

While Jason and Henry were outside looking at the car, Jeanette said to Mary, "Would you like some coffee or a coke?" "Yes, I could drink a cup of coffee." When she returned, she asked Mary, "Have you known Jason very long?" Mary smiled and replied, "For three years. I met him while he was still in prison. I worked there at the prison and sort of fell in love with him." Jeanette grinned and said, "I can see how that could happen."

Once Jason was finished with the paperwork on the car he had just bought, he called the porter into his office and asked him to put Mary's car inside the fence for the night. Mary was looking Jason over from top to bottom.

Until now, Jason had never been to Cheryl's house to pick up James. Margo was out of town for the weekend so he'd have to pick him up this time at Cheryl's house. Jason said he would never go near Cheryl again and the truth was that he didn't want to see her with another man. When he got to Cheryl's house she came to the door and asked, "Jason, how are you?" Jason didn't want to hear her phony small talk so he looked at her and said, "Fine." Just then James came running out the door. Jason smiled at him and said, "Hey son, are you ready to go?" "Yes, sir." James replied. "Good. I hope you got all your toys so you won't be bored." James held up a small bag and said, "I've got all I need daddy. I'm not a kid anymore." Jason looked at Cheryl and said, "I'll have him back by six o'clock on Sunday and tell Margo to call me. I don't like being here."

Jason opened the car door and James climbed into the back seat. Jason said to him, "Son, this is Mary and Mary, this is my son, Mr. James Alan Keeble." Mary smiled at James and said, "Hello James." He looked her over really good, turned to Jason and said, "Daddy, she's prettier than the other girlfriend you have." Mary smiled with embarrassment. "Don't help me, boy," Jason laughed.

Jason was still living at Donna's house which was about thirty minutes away. As they drove along, Jason explained to Mary that Donna was strictly a friend of his and there was no hanky-panky to their relationship. When Jason introduced the two they took an extra minute to look each other over. They soon hit it off well and together prepared a big dinner for everyone while Jason played hide and seek with his son James and Donna's little girl.

After dinner, the kids wanted ice cream so they all went out and within minutes of their returning home, the kids fell asleep. Donna was busy in her room so it was the perfect time for Jason and Mary to talk about old times. Mary was the type of girl that loved to recall old times. She had held back most of her thoughts while she and Jason were together at the prison so this was the perfect time for her to tell Jason how she really felt about him. She truly loved Jason and dreamed of being with him.

Before they knew it, two a.m. was on the clock and Jason said, "Young lady, its bedtime so you've got to make up your mind where you want to sleep." She looked at him and replied, "I want to sleep with you." Jason smiled his little shy smile and said, "Good. I've waited a long time for this day." All that had built up between the two of them was let out that night and Jason used every trick he knew on Mary. She was very experienced in bed as Jason had suspected she would be. Just before daylight, he begged for a break. Mary climbed out of the bed and slipped on his white shirt. Her body was tanned and the white shirt just made her more beautiful. Jason went to the bathroom thinking how exciting she had been. When he came back to the bedroom, she was lying on the bed crying. He was shocked and asked, "Mary, what's the problem? Don't tell me I was that bad in bed." She sniffed her nose and replied, "That's not it at all. Sex with you is wonderful but I know that after last night I will probably never see you again. I love you Jason and I have for a long time. I know I made a mistake getting pregnant and you would never marry me with a child. I can't get away very often to see you but I do wish you would let me come to see you when I can." Jason went back to the bathroom and got a warm cloth to wash her face. Her skin was clear and beautiful. She was the kind of woman he could love but he just couldn't expose her to the things he had to do in life. Besides, she had betrayed him in a small way when she got pregnant. Betrayal was one of his most hated things in life. On the other hand, he wasn't going to spoil their time together so he told her, "Mary, don't cry. You worry too much and you don't know what will happen tomorrow." She smiled at him and said, "I've missed you so much." They talked until she fell asleep but she seemed to be satisfied with seeing him when she could.

When she woke up Jason took her shopping and sent her home with the understanding that she could visit anytime she wanted. Meantime they would talk by phone every week. It was the best way he knew of letting her down without hurting her.

Start where you stand and never mind the past,

The past won't help you in beginning new,

If you have left it all behind at last

Why, that's enough, you're done with it,

You're through.

Berton Braley

14

The years passed with Jason playing a few con games and running the car lot. Jason's partner, Henry, needed his help running the car lot more and more so Jason stayed close by. Business was good and Jason liked having a private office to operate from. It was Nineteen Sixty-Six now and the style of new cars looked better each year, making sales much better and allowing Jason to buy and sell more used cars. He hired a couple of guys from the old days to collect accounts when people didn't make payments on their cars. If they couldn't pay, he would repossess the cars and sell them again.

He was finally off parole and could travel with Cecil when his work at the car lot would permit it. The thing with Mary had now ended with a phone call once or twice a year and he was staying close to Margo.

He and Cecil decided to go out to Texas and play a little con game based on a tip from a friend of Cecil's. Jason couldn't seem to concentrate and told Cecil, "It's time for me to get even with this guy Cheryl married. I owe him one for trying to adopt my son." Cecil replied, "Let it go, Jason, we've got work to do." Jason smiled and said, "The idea I have will take care of my problem with her and the husband and will be a great con game for you and me."

The next week Cheryl received a letter from a law firm in Atlanta, asking her and her husband to visit their offices regarding an important matter. They drove to the office address listed on the letterhead and once inside, a thin, well-dressed man introduced himself, "Mr. and Mrs. Anderson, my name is Rudie Stone. My law firm represents a lady named Rita West. The reason I've asked you here today is because I want to explain a matter that has to do with my client, Miss West, and another man, Jason Keeble. I'll try to explain this in detail but if I go too fast, just stop me." He continued, "Some years back Mr. Keeble and Miss West entered into a joint venture in the nightclub business." The lawyer then produced some documents which he passed to Cheryl. He continued, "As you'll see, the deal was for Mr. Keeble to finance the club in exchange for Miss West running the business. The business ran very well for four years and that's when I got involved. The contract says that, in exchange for managing the place and investing fifteen thousand dollars in the business, Miss West was to acquire fifty percent ownership of the business at the end of five years. If you'll move to paragraph eight..." Cheryl flipped the pages with little interest while her husband looked on. Rudie continued, "This paragraph is very fine print and full of legal jargon but what it boils down to is that Miss West was to put into an escrow account, a certain amount of money each year which, after five years, would be a total of fifteen thousand dollars which would represent her contribution for ownership of half the business. Here is the problem, over the years the building has become run down and needs repairs. In their agreement, Mr. Keeble's lawyer conveniently left out any provisions making him responsible for the upkeep of the building, and now he refuses to pay for the repairs. If she puts up the money for the repairs, she will be short of her investment money necessary to make her a fifty-fifty partner and she will lose what she has worked for all these years. I've filed a law suit on her behalf against Mr. Keeble for planning to steal her half of the business.

Cheryl suddenly blurted out, "Why are you telling us all this? I could care less about Jason's deals." Rudie smiled and replied, "Perhaps so, Mrs. Anderson, but this does concern you. When I'm finished, I think you'll be very glad you took the time to listen. I believe that Mr. Keeble is attempting to swindle my client out of the business and keep her money. I am going to stop him and here is where you stand to gain from this. Next week, Mr. Keeble's business licenses will be up for renewal. I am now furnishing the state licensing board with proof that Mr. Keeble registered the business in the name of your son, James. He used false I.D. for James on the paperwork and no one caught it at the time." The lawyer got out of his seat and walked to the front of his desk, sat on the edge, looked at Cheryl and said, "Here's where you and your husband come into the picture. As long as you don't find out about this, Mr. Keeble's scheme will be safe. My plan is to file a motion in court that says you, Mrs. Anderson, are the legal guardian of your minor child and ask that you be granted full control of any business in your son's name. That will be ordered with no question and at that point, you can step in as your son's guardian and take full control of the business. Once you do this, my client is prepared to continue to fulfill her contract with you. She just wants her fifty percent and to get Keeble out altogether. He has never been any help with the bar and she knows he is going to kick her out and find a new manager. I want to give you the home number for Miss West and have you meet her at the bar to see all that she has worked so hard to build. I have a contract here that I have prepared on behalf of Miss West. In essence, it says exactly what I just explained to you. I'd like to have you study it. I also suggest you let your lawyer go over it. You will own fifty percent of a fifty thousand dollar per year business. The repairs on the building are estimated to be about ten to twelve thousand and she hopes to raise her half of that soon. Cheryl's husband Danny jumped up and quickly agreed to call Rita and take a look at the business.

Cheryl and her husband thanked the lawyer and as the two men shook hands, Rudie said, "Please call me once you meet with Miss West. If you feel good about your meeting, I will file the motion in the courts to get the ball rolling. I want to nail this bastard as hard as I can."

As soon as Cheryl and Danny left the lawyer's office, Danny ran to a pay phone and telephoned Rita West to make an appointment to see the bar. Rita West was sitting by the phone, waiting for the call from Danny. Rita told Danny that Jason was going out of town on Thursday and they could meet at the bar at nine o'clock a.m. She gave them the address and said goodbye. She immediately telephoned Jason and said, "Your guy Danny is jumping up and down to see the bar. Sounds like he really wants to cut your throat." Jason laughed and replied, "They made a big mistake trying to adopt my son and now they have to pay."

On Thursday, Rita was at the bar by eight-thirty a.m. Jason and his friends had put all the right things in the building to make it look like a realistic bar, right down to the sign on the front of the building. When Cheryl and Danny showed up, Rita gave them a great tour of the place and showed them all the repairs that had to be made. She explained that the city inspector had been there and ordered her to close the place until the repairs were made. She then said to Cheryl and Danny, "Jason refused to make the repairs and he will let the place stay closed until I give up and then he will make the repairs and just hire a new manager, and I will lose all that I have put into the place. He is so evil and I really hope you guys can help me get it back open and we can all make money." Rita showed Cheryl and Danny all the receipts for the sales of the past three years and the numbers were very impressive. Rita could see that Danny was getting very excited and was ready to jump right in. Cheryl was very quiet and reserved.

They discussed how the bar would be run and got to know each other. After spending a couple of hours discussing a business plan, they all said goodbye and agreed to talk again soon.

The next day, Cheryl reluctantly agreed to go with her husband to see another lawyer. The lawyer confirmed the contract to be a valid one. He told them that for a five hundred dollar retainer, he would do a full investigation of the business to be sure it was legitimate, but Danny told him he did not want to spend that money, claiming that he had already checked it all out.

That night Cheryl told Danny, "I know Jason much better than you do and he is much smarter than you and this girl Rita and the lawyer are giving him credit for. If this thing is on the up-and-up and we take it from him, he will kill both of us. I really don't want to get involved except to block him from using my son's name." Danny's greed took over and he replied, "Look, Cheryl, you heard our lawyer say the contract was valid and we stand to make twenty-five thousand dollars a year on this deal. Besides, that asshole Jason owes you the money. He paid no child support while he was in prison." Cheryl protested, "I'm telling you, Jason won't take this laying down." Her husband replied, "So what. If he gets near us we'll just call the police and put his sorry ass back where he belongs. I know one of the local detectives and I'll ask him to go see Jason and threaten him. After the threat he made in court, he won't get near us."

That night Cheryl tried to call Jason but she was told that he was out of town for two weeks on business. As Cheryl and her proud husband ate dinner that night she said, "If you think you can outsmart Jason Keeble, you're crazier than I thought. He'll break you and it's all because you want to be a bigger man than he is. I'm against all this. You're going to be sorry." He laughed and told her, "I've got your great con man right where I want him."

The next day, Cheryl and her husband rushed to the lawyer's office to sign the papers that would put Jason out of the business. The lawyer showed Cheryl and Danny the motion he filed to make James the new owner. He explained that Cheryl, being James' guardian, would have full control. He further told them that the judge signed off on it. They left and the lawyer telephoned Jason and said, "Your fish just nibbled on the bait." They laughed and hung up.

Two days later Rita called Cheryl. "We've got a small problem. I just met with the city code enforcement and a contractor and I made a mistake on the cost of the repairs on the building. The code guy is new and is killing me with little things. It looks like we'll each be spending close to twenty-two thousand dollars to make the repairs. I don't have the money but my banker said he would loan me the money if my father puts his house up as collateral. He agreed to help me, so I can get a check for my half." Cheryl thought for a minute then told Rita, "I don't have that kind of money. I think we should just forget all this but I'll tell

Danny what you've told me and we'll get back to you." What Cheryl really wanted to do was just call Jason up and tell him about all this so he could put a stop to it but if her husband found out, he would leave her and she couldn't live on her sole income. Rita ended their conversation by saying, "Cheryl, we have about three days before Jason finds out we forced him out of the business and we should have a plan for when he does. Otherwise, he will try to cause problems. Please get back to me as soon as you can. I am so afraid I'm about to lose all I've worked for."

Cheryl reluctantly gave the news to her husband, relying heavily on the fact they couldn't raise the twenty-two thousand dollars. She told him with a firm hand that the deal was off. He stormed out of the house and came back three hours later. The next day he went to the bank and mortgaged their house, which was solely in his name, and the banker made him the loan. When Cheryl found out, she was furious. She knew he was acting out of pure ego and that Jason would end his little dream really fast.

The next day Cheryl finally agreed to go with Danny to meet Rita at Rudie Stone's office where a contractor showed them plans to remodel the club. It would take him about a month to complete the repairs, unless he had problems. Rita gave Cheryl the blueprints and told her about new bar lights she had plans for. The contractor said he'd start on Monday if all agreed. Cheryl's husband gave the attorney a check for twenty-two thousand dollars made out to Rudie Stone and Cheryl could see the joy it gave him thinking he was about to sink Jason.

On Monday Cheryl and Danny drove out to see how the remodeling was going and the surprise they got was more than they could take. The building was padlocked and had a "NO TRESPASSING" sign on the doors. There was a phone number on the door to call for leasing information. They rushed to a pay phone and found out that a real estate company owned the building. It had previously been rented by a movie company from New York, to be used in making a film. They also called Rudie Stone's office only to find the number there disconnected. They drove to his office and found out it had been rented by the same film company. When they checked further, they found no such film company existed. They ran to the bank to stop payment on the check but it was too late. Of course, Jason had used a false ID bearing the name Rudie Stone to cash the check at the bank earlier that day.

Cheryl cried and cussed all the way home. Danny was so beat, he couldn't even speak. They called the police and an investigation began. Once Cheryl got ahold of her feelings, she knew she needed to talk to Jason. She told her husband she needed some time alone but that she would be back soon. She drove to a pay phone near her house and phoned Jason. When he heard her voice, his first words were, is there a problem with James?" "No," she told him, "Jason how could you do this to us?" Jason replied, "What in the hell are you talking about?" Cheryl stopped crying and said, "You know exactly what I'm talking about." Jason wished she was near him so he could hold her but this was part of the game. She didn't cry when she was trying to take his son away from him so she'd just have to play out the hand. Cheryl explained to Jason what had happened and he denied it all. He said to her, "I'm sure you'd do that to me if you could so maybe you got what you deserved from someone who really wanted to fuck you over."

The next day the police paid Jason a visit. They told him that he would need proof of where he was when all this took place.

Two weeks later, the police told Cheryl and Danny that they had simply been flim-flammed. They told them the investigation would continue but at this point, there was no evidence to lead them to Jason since he never showed his face and his signature was never on any documents. It could have been anyone. Cheryl's husband felt sure Jason would be sent back to prison for this and now he was walking away free as a bird. As Cheryl and Danny lay in bed that night he told her, "I'll kill Jason Keeble."

Soon after, the first payment fell due on the twenty-two thousand dollar mortgage Danny had taken out to fund the bar repairs. Danny had originally been counting on the income from the bar business to make the payments. When Cheryl and Danny couldn't come up with the extra money for the payments, they lost their house in foreclosure and ended up living with Danny's parents. When Jason learned this news, he stared out his office window and thought, "It's the price you pay for trying to take my son from me."

Danny's production at his job fell to nothing due to all the financial pressure he was under. Two months later, he was asked to resign. He was almost at his breaking point. Jason decided to ask the courts to give James to him until Cheryl was more financially stable. However, before the papers were filed, things took a drastic change.

It was Friday and Cheryl drove to the car lot with James. Jason had gone to the other side of town to pay off some cars and bid on some others. Jason's secretary welcomed Cheryl and James into the office. Soon Jason and the porter returned to the lot. The secretary met Jason at the door and told him, "You've got company. It's James and his mother." When Jason went into his office he found James playing with Jason's business partner Henry while Cheryl sat by the window. He was surprised to see Cheryl there. "What could she be up to?" He had told her months back to never set foot on his lot. He spoke up and said, "Well, this looks like a nice little party." Then he turned to Henry and said, "Henry, I bought one old truck and three cars today. They'll deliver them tomorrow. I also paid off all the other cars we sold last week." He then turned to James and said, "How are you son?" James replied, "I'm fine, daddy, we're spending the weekend with you." Jason looked at Cheryl with a very puzzled look and said, "That's nice to hear." Then he turned to Henry and said, "Henry, why don't you take James outside for a while and let me talk to Cheryl." Henry said, "Sure Jason." He turned to James and continued, "Come on boy, I've put something new on the race car. Let me show it to you."

Jason took off his coat, poured himself a drink and sat down behind his desk. He didn't say a word to Cheryl. He just stared at her. She looked more scared than he'd ever seen her but still as beautiful as ever. He finally broke the silence saying, "What in the hell are you doing here?

We agreed that you would never come here." She looked at him with tears in her eyes and replied, "Jason, I've got a lot of problems and we need to talk." He replied, "We could have talked on the phone and if you have problems they're of no concern to me." She answered, "I know that. I expected you to be this way, but I need to leave James with you for a week or so until I get some things put back together. You...or somebody...ruined me and Danny. I should have stopped it but Danny thought he could break you and because of his stupidity, I've left him." Jason smiled and said, "You know, I don't think you left him because of his stupidity. My guess is that you left him for the same reason you left me. When a man runs out of money you're through with him." Cheryl jumped from her seat and said, "Jason, I didn't come here to argue with you. I left Glenda and Angie with their father and James wanted to stay with you." He could tell Cheryl was completely out of control, and quite naturally, his heart softened. He asked, "Have you had lunch?" "No." She replied. He buzzed his secretary and asked her to make a reservation for two at MiMi's restaurant downtown.

As they were driving out of the parking lot, Jason heard the race car start up. He and Henry, along with some help from James had built a dirt track racer and played with it on the weekends. James loved the car and drove his mother crazy talking about it. She didn't quite believe many of the tales her son had told her about driving the car. At thirteen, how much driving could he do? Suddenly the car came rumbling out of the garage with James at the wheel. Cheryl almost fainted. He drove past them, turned it around and came back by. As he passed Jason's car he revved the engine up and shot his mother and father a big boastful smile. Jason rolled the window down and yelled to him, "Boy, I'm going to kill you for playing with that car." James yelled back, "Daddy, I'm just getting it out to wash it and I had to get close to the hose pipe." Jason shrugged and said, "Sure, sure. Hurry up and shut it off. Your mother and I will be back soon. You stay here with Henry." As Cheryl and Jason drove away she said, "Jason please tell me that you didn't teach James to drive that car." He replied, "No, it was Henry who did that and we're very careful about him driving so don't worry about it." Driving a car was a small trick compared to a few of the little con games James had picked up but Jason couldn't let Cheryl know about that.

Cecil had won the deed to a small grocery store in a poker game and he gave it to Jason with the understanding that it would be given to Jason's three kids when they were of age. Jason decided to hire an old man to run the place. This man had owned a store for thirty years and was now in retirement. The old man's name was Al so they named the store "Big Al's Grocery." On the way to lunch with Cheryl, Jason stopped to leave some cash at the store to pay a few bills and this would be a good time to let Cheryl see her son's first business. She had also heard a lot of stories about the store.

Once inside, Cheryl saw a very large, broad-shouldered, well-dressed older man sitting in a big rocker near an old pot-bellied heater. Jason said to him, "Hello Al, how are you today?" The old man looked up with a smile and said, "Fine young man and how is your day going?" Jason replied, "I'm good. Just wish I had your job." They both laughed. Al was a good-hearted old countryman who took very good care of the store. Everything was very neat and in its place and the store had the smell of fresh cheese pouring out the door. Jason went on, "Jeanette asked me to leave two hundred dollars with you to pay the beer bill and the light bill." "Yes, sir. She called me and said you'd be coming by." Jason walked to the rear of the store where he had put in a separate counter for a hamburger stand. He had hired a guy named Charlie to run the stand on a percentage basis and it was doing well. Jason said to him, "Hello Charlie." He was busy cooking and without looking up, he yelled, "Hello Jason. Would you like a hamburger on the house?" "No thanks, I'm on my way to lunch now." Jason liked to associate himself with the employees on a regular basis. He had learned while he was in the drug business that a personal relationship with the employees would keep them loyal. Cheryl was wandering around the store when Jason said, "Hey guys, this lady with me is James' mother, Cheryl." Both men said hello to her and bragged about what a good kid James was. They also reminded her of how much like his father he had become. She wasn't crazy about that thought.

During lunch, Jason and Cheryl talked about the old times when they were together. Jason had already decided to help her financially but he didn't know why. He invited her to stay the night with him and James so she could clear up her head. She accepted and confessed that it was her reason for coming to him personally in the first place. She looked relieved but Jason wasn't sure what she might do in the long run. There had been a lot of distrust between the two of them.

After lunch, she spent the rest of the day just hanging around the car lot. Jason showed her everything. He even tried to get her to take a ride in the race car with James but she refused that ride in a hurry.

That evening they all drove to an old building that Jason had renovated. It was an old barn sitting under some large oak trees about five hundred yards off the main road. Jason had spotted it one day and had to have it. He'd spent a lot of money making it into a home but he loved it and especially the peace and quiet. Cheryl looked shocked when they pulled in but it was just as James had described it to her. As she walked in, the entrance was a wide hallway with a very rustic brick floor. It was covered with large green plants, antiques and two slow moving ceiling fans. At the end of the hallway, there were two steps down that led into a large den. It was decorated with more antiques and a large fireplace. There were two large windows on each side of the fireplace that looked out over a large pasture and lake. The deck on the back of the house stretched from one side to the other. Jason kept a maid there all the time and James ran to her for his usual hug. He then grabbed his mother's hand and took her on a long tour of the entire house. She was very impressed but not surprised.

Jason always had to have the best of everything. When the tour was over Jason called the housekeeper and asked her to start dinner. James called out to the housekeeper, "Please set another place, my mother is staying here tonight." The meal was wonderful and for the first time in weeks, Cheryl relaxed and enjoyed her food without being sick. After dinner, they all got comfortable in the den to watch a movie. James soon fell asleep and the housekeeper put him to bed in his room and settled into her room for the night. Jason and Cheryl talked for hours. Jason never confessed to taking everything she and her husband had but did have a good laugh about the husband threatening to kill him.

The next day was Saturday and when Cheryl woke up, Jason had already left for work. Martha, the housekeeper, and James had left a note saying they had gone to town to do some shopping. It gave Cheryl a chance to prowl around the house. In one bedroom she found a large painting of herself on the wall and around the room were other things that belonged to them when they were married. She smiled and thought, "I guess he really did love me." She spent the rest of the day just relaxing and thinking about where her life might go next.

That evening Jason sent a guy who worked for him to the house who told Cheryl to put on some jeans. He said, "Jason wants you to bring James and come meet him." They drove to the local race car track where they met Jason and Henry. They drove straight into the pit where all the race cars were parked and Cheryl was amazed at all the noise. She could tell that they were all into the racing thing and James was like a kid in a candy store. They let James drive the car onto and off of the trailer and help them work on it. Larry was the major driver but Jason and Henry couldn't resist getting under the wheel and James stood on top of the trailer cheering as loud as he could when his dad was driving. Cheryl watched Jason's driver, Larry, and couldn't help thinking she knew him from somewhere. Then it came to her that he was one of Jason's bodyguards from the old days.

When she mentioned it to Jason, he told her she was mistaken and not to bring it up again. Henry let James back the race car off of the trailer while Cheryl screamed about how he could be killed. Henry was the mechanic and they were all excited about the racing business. It also kept Jason's mind off the road. As Cheryl watched everyone working on the car she thought, "Why couldn't Jason have been this kind of man when I was married to him instead of chasing the bars and girls all the time."

The races ended around one o'clock in the morning. They came in third place but that was fine for Jason. He just enjoyed the rush he got from driving and he did have a few female fans that made a big fuss over him. Cheryl noticed that. Everybody dozed on the way home, except Jason and Cheryl. They talked about the racing and she felt more relaxed than she had in a long time. By the time they got home and got James settled, Jason was beat. He said goodnight to Cheryl, took a shower and went straight to bed. Cheryl soon showed up at his door with the excuse that she couldn't sleep and he decided maybe he wasn't as sleepy as he thought. It had been a long time since he'd touched her. He had to destroy a man in order to be with her but for Cheryl's love, a man would do anything and Jason was no exception. When the sun came up, they were just getting to sleep. Without knowing it, they were in love again and Jason thought, "I guess I'll always love her."

Cheryl, James and her daughters moved in with Jason the next day. In three months, Jason and Cheryl were married again. The day before the wedding, Jason told Cheryl he had business to take care of but he would be home soon. He went straight to Margo's house and she was very excited to see him as always. She never chased Jason. She knew that would crowd him so she just waited patiently for him to contact her. She was all over him until he said, "Margo, I'm here with bad news and I'm sorry but I have to do this." "What Jason? What is wrong? You look sick. Is someone hurt?" "No." he replied. "You will think I've lost my mind but tomorrow I'm marrying Cheryl again." Margo almost fainted. She begged him not to do it but he explained how it was affecting James and her daughters and how happy they all were. Margo finally said, "Jason I think it's all for the wrong reason but I do understand and just know I'll always be here for you no matter what you do. I've always loved you and I always will." Jason said good night but assured Margo he would still drop by from time to time.

The wedding was kept very low key with friends and family. They left the kids with the housekeeper and flew to New Orleans where their days were spent shopping and their nights walking in the famous French Quarter.

On Saturday morning when Cheryl awoke, Jason was putting on a suit. She yawned and asked, "Where are you going? It's our honeymoon." Never looking up, he replied, "I've got a little business to take care of this morning." Cheryl had almost forgotten about Jason's old con games and as she lay there watching him finish dressing, she decided it was time for her to face the fact that he had to play those games or he wouldn't be Jason.

Jason rented a limousine and driver to take him to a breakfast house on the outskirts of town where he was to meet a man for a ten a.m. appointment. He had found an ad in the paper where someone wanted to sell an expensive diamond ring so he decided to take a look at it. When he arrived, the man was already there and was impressed when Jason pulled up in a limo. The man introduced himself as Bill Sims. They had coffee and some small talk, then Sims showed Jason the diamond ring. It was a beautiful three carat solitaire and appeared to be very real. Jason looked at the ring closely but even more so, studied the guys face to see how anxious he was to sell the ring and for more than he paid for it new. Jason loved a greedy man. He returned the ring to Sims and said, "How much Mr. Sims?" Sims drew a long breath and replied, "Seven thousand dollars. It appraises for twelve thousand five." Jason was quiet for a solid minute watching Sim's face, then he said, "I like it and I want it. It's for my sister and new brother-in-law. They are getting married and can't afford much so I want to give them something nice. I do need him to see it but it's free to him so how could he not like it." They laughed and Jason could see the guy sweating as he envisioned Jason buying that diamond. Jason said, "My brother-in-law will be in town tonight. We have business near here." They made a deal to meet at the same place about one p.m. the next day to close the deal. As Sims drove away, he glanced down at a business card Jason had given him which read, "Southeastern Drilling and Exploring Company, Dallas, Texas. Richard Jackson, President." Sims smiled and thought, "This guy didn't even question the price. But from the looks of that limo he was in and the suit he was wearing, I'd say he can afford whatever he wants."

The next morning, Jason was up early and off to the airport where he met his friend Larry who had flown in from back home. Larry was wearing a three-piece suit and looked very professional. They made small talk as they drove to the restaurant where they met their "mark". Jason greeted Sims saying, "Mr. Sims, this is my brother-in-law, Larry Turner. Did you bring the ring?" Sims shook hands with Larry and replied, "I sure did." With that, he took the ring from his coat pocket. They all sat down and Jason showed the ring to Larry asking, "How's that for a rock, pal?" Larry took the ring and looked it over carefully. Sims was smiling with pride but Larry would soon put a stop to all that. Larry looked at Jason and said, "Mr. Jackson, the ring is beautiful but why do you show it to me?"

Jason looked at him grinning and replied, "It's a surprise for you and my sister. You can add a band and use it as a wedding ring." Larry looked very surprised and said, "Mr. Jackson, I really appreciate all you do for us but that ring is far more than I can afford right now." The mark almost hit the floor. Here was Jason already saying he wanted it and now some punk is trying to mess things up. Jason spoke up and said, "Look Larry, you're marrying into a family that doesn't think about the price of things, we just get what we want." The color finally came back into Sims face but the argument between Jason and Larry went on until Jason was angry almost to the point of yelling. He calmed down and said to Larry, "Look, boy, I don't need your approval to buy my sister a ring. I just wanted to know what you thought of it. Did you bring the envelope I called and asked you to bring for Mr. Sims here?"

Larry looked out the window in disgust and replied, "Yes I did." He then reached into his pocket and produced a small envelope. Along with a second larger envelope. He handed the large envelope to Jason and said, "Before I forget, the office wants you to sign these contracts and send them back tonight by courier." As Sims looked on, Jason took the small envelope and laid it aside. He then took the large envelope with the contracts and said to Sims, "Excuse me for just a minute." He pretended to read the contract, making sure Sims saw the pages as he laid them on the table one at a time. Then he turned to Larry and said in a loud voice, "Are these fucking people crazy? I told them I'd do that drilling for two hundred thousand dollars and this contract says one hundred fifteen thousand. I'm not signing this shit. I'll deal with this once we get back to Dallas." He tossed the contract aside and reached for the small envelope. He opened it and produced a cashier's check for seven thousand dollars. He handed it to the mark and said, "Mr. Sims, I apologize to you for getting you tied up in the middle of family business. If you'll accept this check on my bank, I'll be happy to buy the ring from you." Jason had cussed and made such a scene until Sims was now intimidated by him. He took a quick look at the cashier's check, handed Jason the ring and said his goodbyes to them both.

Jason and Larry had a cup of coffee with doughnuts and drove back to the hotel where Cheryl was waiting. In two hours they were all on a plane to Atlanta. Once there, Jason stopped by a friend's house that was a fence for stolen merchandise. He sold the ring to the fence for thirty-five hundred dollars. When Mr. Sims went to the bank in New Orleans with the cashier's check, he was told that it was counterfeit.

Time passed with Jason playing a few con games but staying close to home and running the car lot as much as possible. Things were good between him and Cheryl. When Jason was on the road, Cheryl would busy herself by helping Jeanette run the office at the car lot.

Everything was going exactly the way Cheryl wanted until she woke up from a nap on the sofa at their house to overhear Jason explaining, in detail, a con game to James. Cheryl came unglued, screaming and yelling until she and Jason had their first serious fight since the reconciliation. She told him she would never condone her son being taught that life. Jason blew her off and left the house mad.

James was sixteen now and could run the car lot almost by himself. He drove the race car now at almost every race and made huge decisions about the business. Jason had taught him well. It made Cheryl sick to see how much her son was growing up to be like his father. She had much bigger plans for him. When James was with his father, he'd beg to go on the road with him and learn all the games. Jason knew that would be a very sensitive matter with Cheryl, so he'd have to break her into the traveling very slowly.

The more Cheryl bitched about Jason teaching James tricks, the more upset she made him. James liked the cons but actually spent most of his time with Cecil learning how to be a good poker player. When James turned seventeen, Jason took him on a road trip without saying a word to anyone. Their first stop was the local library where they used the typewriter to type different addresses on forty envelopes. They drove to a small town in Florida and found the local post office there. Jason went in and bought a three dollar money order, put it in an empty envelope and sealed it up. He explained to James what he was about to do as they drove ten miles to the next town. Again he found the local post office and said to James, "Give me a minute to get inside and drift in behind me. Pay close attention to what I do and say." Once inside, Jason said hello to the clerk and pulled out a roll of money which consisted of twenties, fives and a bunch of ones. He then said to the clerk, "I need a money order for three hundred dollars please." She made out the money order and gave it to Jason as he passed the money to her. As she counted the money, Jason pulled an envelope from his pocket, pretended to write on the money order and placed it in the envelope. As he licked the envelope he said, "I don't know which is the hardest, licking the envelope or paying my alimony." They both laughed. He made sure she saw him seal it up and place it in his right hip pocket.

Suddenly she stopped counting and said, "I'm sorry sir but you've only got two hundred and ninety-three dollars here." Jason looked at her puzzled and said, "What? I was sure there were three hundred dollars here. I even threw in two extra dollars for the price of the money order." The lady pushed all the money toward Jason saying, "You're welcome to count it, sir." Jason stared at the money for a second then reached into his pocket and pulled out the envelope with the three dollar money order in it. He then picked up the money from the counter and handed the envelope to the cashier. He said to her, "You hang on to this envelope while I get more money from my wallet. It's in my car. I'll be right back." As he walked out, the clerk held the envelope up to the light and saw the money order inside it. James was standing behind Jason looking bored and as she looked at the envelope, he got her attention and bought a book of stamps.

Jason and James then drove to the local liquor store cashed the money order for three hundred dollars and bought a quart of Scotch. When they didn't return to the post office, the lady gave the envelope to the post master general. There was a law that only the post master general could open a piece of sealed mail. When he opened the letter he found the three dollar money order and after the clerk explained what happened, he told her that she had been the victim of some slick con artist.

Jason and James went all the way to California playing that game and along the way, he taught James several other games. "Using different games," he told James, "stops the police from seeing a pattern and knowing where you are." As they traveled, Jason found them the finest women to spend time with and James loved it. After three weeks Jason said to James, "Son, take us back to Atlanta. I'm homesick." James was a natural like his father and didn't need much training to catch on to the games but as they drove home, Jason wasn't sure how proud he was of teaching his son the cons. He was, however, sure that he and Cheryl would have big trouble over this little trip.

When they got home, Cheryl calmly asked Jason for a divorce. He didn't argue with her. He gave the car lot to James and Henry, the house to Cheryl, along with a job for her at the car lot and enough money for her and James to live on for the next five years. He then packed his clothes and went home to his true love, the life of a con man.

He found an apartment he could use when he was in town and he visited the kids every time he could. He sat down and explained his love of the games to the kids and they understood as much as they could. They still loved their father very much and he helped them every time he could. Elizabeth, his oldest daughter married and became the chorus teacher at a local college. His youngest, Cindy was pursuing an acting career and running wild like Jason did at her age. James was taking care of the car lot and the grocery store. He and Jason also made sure his step-sisters had the things they needed.

James started to gamble like his grandfather and loved it. No traveling and lots of fun and money. He could play the suckers and stay close to home. He soon met a young girl named Charlotte. She was a very calm girl with long red hair and she worshiped James. When he announced their plans for marriage Cheryl was overjoyed and planned a small wedding as Charlotte had asked her to do. She had everything done beautifully. The wedding was a great reunion for the family. Cheryl and Jason barely spoke but then, Jason did bring three young blondes with him, so how could a person blame Cheryl.

Life is short. Break the rules.

Forgive quickly. Kiss SLOWLY.

Love truly. Laugh uncontrollably.

And never regret ANYTHING

that makes you smile.

Mark Twain

15

A heart attack at age forty-seven didn't surprise Jason at all. After all, there were times when his heart seemed to actually stop beating during some of his games. "It's time you rest," his doctor told him. "Go somewhere quiet and relax. Take it easy for the next two years or you won't make it even one more year."

After some searching, Jason landed in the small town of Kessler, Georgia, seventy-five miles south of Atlanta. Nobody would know him there. The town was quiet and near enough to Atlanta for him to drive there when he needed to feed the addiction he had for the city. That addiction seemed to own his soul throughout the years. He went to Atlanta once long ago as a young man to play a con game and the city overpowered him, body and soul. He loved the feeling and never called anywhere else home. It was also close to where his kids lived so he could visit them when he was home.

After deciding to live in Kessler during his two years rest, he drove back to Atlanta to see his old girlfriend Margo. He'd always had a very special place for her in his heart and spent time with her when he could. He told her of his health problems and asked if she'd go to Kessler with him and pose as his wife for the next two years. Her life had been plain and simple so the offer to be with Jason for the next two years thrilled her. She thought, "I'm sure there will be plenty of excitement in it." Thanks to the money Jason had sent Margo, she had retired from her job and was living off of the investments he had helped her get into so she had no ties to Atlanta. She'd fallen in love with Jason the first time they met but knew they could never be married as long as he was in love with Cheryl and to her it was obvious that he was. She packed and wondered, "Could he finally be over her now? Just where could this end up?" They drove to see another friend of Jason's who provided them with papers that gave them both new names and that day they became Mr. and Mrs. Christopher and Vicki Reynolds which was okay with Margo. She loved the idea that he would be hers for the next two years.

Once Mr. and Mrs. Reynolds picked out a house, Jason called a friend who handled his money to come down and close the deal. The house was deeded to a private investment firm which Jason's accountant created. His money had become a problem for him over the years. He only needed enough to set up his next game so the accountant invested the money and it had grown to a figure that Jason couldn't believe. The guy was a good friend of Jason's from the old days and he kept the IRS off Jason's back. He also eliminated the worry of where to keep all the money Jason had made over the years, which now totaled near three million dollars. The only concern Jason had was to make sure the kids got their regular allotments. He tried to keep them humble but he always got weak when they needed something. Jason's son, James, was

now twenty-three years old. Like his father, James had learned the cons very well but preferred betting on sports games. James was still wet behind the ears and needed lots of money to support his family and his womanizing. His mother, Cheryl, was trying to keep close tabs on the money from the car lot but James had the last say on that. She didn't know he was relying heavily on the money he

James

182

money he made from gambling.

With two years of time on his hands, Jason planned to busy himself with ideas for new con games. That should keep him occupied. After all, he of all people knew how to do time. He and Margo found the perfect house just off the city square downtown. Margo fixed it up nicely. Jason didn't care much about the house. He only required that it have a large den where he could spend some time alone.

Weeks passed with them hardly leaving the house except to buy groceries and visit the kids. Margo loved it. It was like really being married. One day Jason needed some cigars, a new habit he acquired. As he stopped at the store in town for his regular brand, he overheard the storekeeper talking to a flashy man. Jason learned the man was Joe Pollard, the Mayor of Kessler. The storekeeper said to him, "Mayor Pollard, I'd like to support the new factory you plan to build. I know it's for the good of the city but my money is short right now. I operated in the red all last year." Mayor Pollard was a man who could easily intimidate people and no one liked being bullied by him. Jason thought, "This guy Pollard would be a real mark and he appears to have a lot of money. I'll have to remember him." The Mayor and storekeeper talked for a while and finally, a generous donation of five hundred dollars was made by the storekeeper. Jason wondered what kind of pressure had been used on the poor man. As Jason paid for the cigars, the storekeeper said, "You're Mr. Reynolds who just moved into the old house on View Pointe Lane, right?" Jason smiled, remembering small town gossip, and replied, "Yes I am." "Well, how do you like our fine city?" Jason replied, "It's a good place for a man to retire." Jason thanked the man for the cigars and as he was walking out the door the old storekeeper said to him, "Welcome to Kessler, Mr. Reynolds, and feel free to stop in my store anytime." "Thank you." Jason replied. Once outside the store, Jason thought, "The old guy was just pressured to give up five hundred dollars, yet he bounced back with a big smile for me like it happens every day. He'd be another good mark I could beat easily."

Jason knew he could tell a lot about the cash flow in a town by running a fast game on a local shop owner and while he certainly would love to get a check on this little town, he had promised himself that he wouldn't con anyone while he lived here.

Jason soon got to know all of the local businessmen very well. They grew to like his style and would often ask for his advice on money matters regarding their businesses. Jason eventually found out that this quiet little town had more money in it than he ever imagined. But worse, it was as if they didn't know what to do with it, except hand it over to this guy Pollard for some new project to "improve" the city.

Mayor Pollard seemed to control everything and not by being nice. He simply bullied everyone and they gave in to him. Jason didn't like Pollard and he avoided him.

During the first year Jason was there, it seemed that whenever he went into town, more and more people would stop him and ask him for advice on some business issues. He would listen and make suggestions on ways to hike sales and motivate employees. Jason had a natural talent for running a business and they saw it. He was always a good judge of people. The businessmen started seeing him as a financial wizard. He thought to himself, "Every man in this town is so naive about the business world they wouldn't even recognize bad advice."

Mayor Pollard soon learned of Jason's popularity with the people and saw it as a threat to himself and his control over the city. He decided that it was time for Jason to move on. He tried telling Jason about great business investments in the larger cities, in hopes that Jason would pack up and leave. Jason laughed at him. That made Pollard furious so he bought the house next door to Jason and moved a black family named Salter in; that should do it. Pollard was sure this would drive Jason from the neighborhood. But the next day Jason saw to it that an article ran in the society section of the local paper about the Salter family coming to dinner at Jason and Margo's home. It read:

Mr. and Mrs. Christopher Reynolds entertained Mr. and Mrs. Willie Salter with a festive evening of cocktails and dinner at their home on Sunday.

Pollard's resentment grew. He wanted Jason out of Kessler and he would stop at nothing to make him leave. Little did Pollard know that Jason was getting cabin fever and thinking about leaving. Jason would never reveal to Pollard that he was having any thoughts of leaving because he had made a game of agitating Pollard.

By the end of Jason's first full year of "Retirement," as he called it, he was enjoying the simple life but also missing the road and the games. He decided it was time to move on, doctor's orders or not. He had to break the news to Margo and he dreaded that part. He asked her to join him for a nice quiet meal at their favorite restaurant in Atlanta. She always enjoyed dressing up and going out with Jason. After a pleasant dinner together, Jason shared his plan with Margo and she was shocked. She knew that there was no need to try and change his mind. She was sad but understood. They decided she should move back into her house in Atlanta. Jason had paid off the mortgage on her house and promised he would keep her financially secure for the rest of her life. Margo had always been there for him and had proven herself to be his best friend. Of all the women in and out of Jason's life, Margo would probably be the one he would want to grow old with. But for now, he had nothing on his mind but the road and some new con games he had been working on. As they drove back to Kessler, they anticipated a calm night to prepare for the changes taking place, but when they turned onto their street the surprise they got was more than they could believe. Their house was burning to the ground. The neighbors had gathered around while the fire truck sprayed water on the charred remains of the house. Jason couldn't imagine this happening just as he was planning to leave town. He questioned his new neighbor, Willie Salter, who was watching as the fire was being put out. After a few words with him, Jason had a pretty good idea that Salter knew who was behind this fire. Salter was way too nervous and couldn't look Jason in the eye. The old man who ran the store where Jason bought his cigars, saw Jason and Willie Salter talking. He slipped Jason a piece of paper and the words were scribbled on it, "YOUR NEXT DOOR NEIGHBOR WILLIE SALTER IS POLLARD'S RIGHT HAND MAN. I THOUGHT YOU KNEW THAT."

The next day people from all over the city came by the hotel where Jason and Margo were staying to offer help and say how sorry they were for the fire. Margo truly was saddened by the fire because she had lost precious old photographs.

Jason had previously given one of the local realtors some tips on real estate deals so the realtor told Jason he'd give him a good deal on another house. Everybody begged Jason not to leave. They knew he was the only hope for them to make changes in their town. Jason told the realtor, "Thank you, but I've already found the house I want."

Jason told Margo he'd changed his mind about leaving Kessler and they'd stay in the hotel for the next thirty days. Meanwhile, Jason got in touch with his old con partner, Lenny Patillo, who had made parole from prison. "Hey pal," Jason told Lenny, "I've got a mark I want to play and with your help I think he'll buy the quit claim game real fast." It would take Lenny a couple of days to get to town and get set up, giving Jason time to make sure his hunch was right. Jason asked his friend at the realty company to research the title on the house next door that Salter lived in. Just as Jason suspected, the title was registered to Willie Salter and was clear and free of any debt. Coincidentally, the deed was registered to Salter only three days after Jason's house burned. Further checking, the realtor found records showing the house had previously belonged to Pollard. Jason suspected Pollard gave Salter the house as payment for setting the fire. Jason's mind raced with the thought, "Pollard, all this to drive me out of town. If only you had known I was about to leave anyway. Now you have to pay."

The next day Jason drove to Atlanta to meet Lenny and set up the con. It was the first time Jason had seen Lenny since they were in jail together. They had lots to talk about. Jason told Lenny about Salter burning down his house and said, "This little con game should break

Salter, and I'll take care of you."

That night Jason showed up at the local pool hall. He passed a tip to a black guy nicknamed "Stick" whom he'd seen hanging out with Salter. Jason told Stick about a big poker game that was happening soon where there would be a lot of money and a bunch of real suckers. He showed Stick the two thousand dollars he had won the night before and told him that he only needed to take a friend who knew how to stack the cards. Stick bought the setup and shot straight to Salter with the idea. Salter never bothered to ask Stick where he got the tip.

When Salter and Stick showed up at the game, Lenny recognized them right away and signaled the guys at the table. The place Lenny had rented was a large house just outside of Atlanta that was quiet and would be perfect for the game. They welcomed Salter and Stick. After everybody was introduced, Stick spoke up and said, "I'm not really a good poker player so I may just hang out with Salter." Then Lenny told Stick, "If you're not going to play, then why don't we let you be our dealer." Salter wanted to jump for joy at that suggestion because not only was Stick a great poker player, he was a pro at stacking a deck. As the game started, Salter could see right away that these guys had more money than they did brains. Little did he know, these were among the top poker players in the country and Salter never saw the setup coming. Four hours later Salter was winning fifteen thousand dollars and he could do no wrong with Stick being able to stack the cards and deal off the bottom.

Finally, one of the guys at the table said, "I've only got about another thirty minutes to play and I've got to leave." The other guys all acknowledged him saying, "We're so deep in now that we can't leave. We've got to go for broke." Salter loved hearing that and he'd help them out. When most of the money was finally in Salter's hands, someone came out with the deed to a forty-two-foot boat and another guy said he had land to put up. Lenny said he thought the boat was worth about forty-five thousand and the land was worth thirty-two thousand. Another guy put up his dairy farm which was worth fifty thousand and said, "This should be enough money to play all night." Lenny showed everyone quit claim deeds, explained how they work and everyone except Salter signed one. Sweat broke out on Salter's face after that move.

There were thousands there for the taking. Then one of the guys spoke up and said, "I really don't want the lucky nigger to play anymore tonight." He knew that using the "n" word would upset Salter and part of the strategy of a good poker player is to upset your opponent. The word really meant nothing to him. Another guy said, "I say he stays but he has to match our ante or get out." At first, Salter and Stick were angry and wanted to leave but they had won seventeen thousand and hated to quit. Salter spoke up saying, "I shouldn't have to match any pot. I've got plenty of money." One of the guys interrupted him saying, "Then get the hell out." Lenny wasn't worried about Salter and Stick leaving with the money; if they didn't stay, Lenny and the other guys would just rob them both and send them on their way. Salter knew he owned his house by all legal rights so he'd simply put it up and take the rest of these chumps' money. No one would ever know what he did.

Salter then signed a quit claim deed. The highly skilled poker players knew that Stick had been stacking the deck all night which was part of their big plan. Just as the game was about to begin, one of the players interrupted by bringing out a new deck of cards and said, "With the stakes this high, we take turns dealing from here on out." Salter almost fell out of his chair but knew that making a big deal over Stick not being the dealer could alert the other players that he and Stick had been cheating.

They agreed to keep the ante the same and for the next nine hours, they went up and down with the big pots until the gamblers knew Stick and Salter were tired and exhausted from sitting there all night. By the time the sun came up the next morning, Salter was dead broke.

His mind raced with the thought that he had lost his house and his wife would be furious. He also remembered that he owed Pollard fifteen thousand dollars cash he had borrowed. He thought to himself

"Facing my wife with no home and Pollard with no money is more that I want to deal with." He begged the other gamblers for enough money to get home which he used to buy a bus ticket to New York where he had relatives. He never returned to Kessler.

Later at the pool room, Sitck confessed to Jason that the guys were real idiots but Salter had just gotten greedy and tried to play too long. His luck turned and he lost it all. Jason said, "I'll let you know when they are playing again; maybe you can get even." Stick replied, "Thank you but I sure won't be interested in a game like that and Salter has left town and made me promise to never tell where he is."

Lenny drove to Kessler the next week where he met with Jason and signed the quit claim for Willie Salter's house over to him. They met with the real estate agent and Lenny sold it to Jason for what appeared to be thirty thousand dollars. Actually, Lenny only took ten thousand from Jason which was payment to the other gamblers for their time.

The next week Jason had Salter's wife moved out of the house and gave her enough money to rent a cheaper place for herself and her kids. Then Jason and Margo did some work on the house and moved into it. When Jason finally came face to face with Pollard, he smiled thinking, "You bastard, you're next." Pollard was certain that Jason had something to do with Salter's disappearance but he couldn't figure out what. When Pollard found out Jason had bought Salter's house, he was furious and swore to get even with Jason. Little did he know that he was no match for Jason Keeble.

The city election for mayor came up soon after the fire and everybody knew that no one would challenge Pollard. Then one of the city councilmen suggested finding someone to run against Pollard and all eyes went to the fine Mr. Reynolds. After all, he'd brought wealth to the city for more than a year now.

Soon, more than a hundred people called the city council to nominate Mr. Reynolds as city mayor. When Jason was confronted with the news and why the people wanted him, he felt badly. He knew the people needed his help but he couldn't stay there and be the mayor even if he wanted to. Mr. Jones, the head of the city council told Jason, "Mr. Reynolds, we need to take the power and control of this city away from Pollard. We need a new hospital and Pollard takes all our funds to build some factory that makes no one money but him. Won't you please help us?" Jason knew they needed help and he hated to turn his back on them so he told them, "Gentlemen, I need some time to think about this."

For the next four days, Jason spent most of his time at home. Margo was sure he had been faced with a big decision but no matter what, she knew he would make Pollard sorry for what he had done. Then one night during dinner Jason said to Margo, "I've got a plan to get even with Pollard. If you don't mind I'd like for you to go out tomorrow and buy yourself some new clothes. You're going to become the new mayor's wife." Margo laughed but she knew Pollard would be sorry when Jason got through with him.

After dinner, Jason dialed the phone at his son's house. When a female voice answered, He asked, "Is this my favorite daughter-in-law?" Charlotte laughed and said, "Daddy I'm your only daughter-in-law. How are you doing?" Jason said, "I'm great for an old man. Where is that no-good son of mine?" "He's in the den," she replied. "The guys are over here playing poker." Jason said, "Would you please ask him to take a break and come to the phone. It's important." When James answered the phone, Jason said, "Son, could you please put your wife in the car this Saturday night and drive to my house. I've decided to run for mayor of this little town and I want to have a little celebration."

Revenge is a dish which taste best when served cold.

Mario Puzo

At least I have the flowers of myself,

And my thoughts,

no God can take that;

I have the fervor of myself for a presence

and my own spirit for light...

Before I am lost,

hell must open like a red rose

for the dead to pass.

Barbara Guest

16

As James and Charlotte were driving to Kessler, James said, "My dad says he's settling down to become the mayor of this little town he's living in. I don't believe he'll ever settle down until he finds that million dollar con game he's always talked about."

After a warm reception and dinner with his son and daughter-in-law, Jason took James into the study where they stayed for the next three hours. Jason explained to James at great length that he wanted to settle down and marry Margo. Being mayor would allow him to be calm and help these people. It would also make him feel good about some things he had done in the past.

James said, "I must tell you that all this is a big surprise to me and you sound very serious but I have to ask, how can you become mayor under a fictitious name?" Jason replied, "I've thought about that. I'm talking to my attorney and he says that the Reynolds name he got for me is someone who works for him and I can use it for as long as I need to." James smiled and said, "That works for me. I will miss my dad!" They laughed.

When James and Charlotte were getting ready to leave, Jason said, "Son, I need your help and support to make this happen so I hope that I can count on you." James looked at Charlotte and replied, "I think she won't mind me helping an old man cross the road." They all laughed except for Jason and he was mumbling something under his breath about, "I'm forty-nine and I can still kick your little punk ass."

The next week James showed up at the Kessler city courthouse wearing a new blue suit. He asked to see the head of the city council. The lady at the front desk said, "That would be Mr. Jones. May I give him your name?" James produced a business card and replied, "My name is James Benton." When James went into Mr. Jones' office he had no problems deciding the man was very meek and very concerned about the future of the city. James said to him, Mr. Jones, I received a call from Mr. Christopher Reynolds asking me to manage his campaign in the race for mayor of your city and I'm here to discuss the details with you." Jones picked up the phone and asked his secretary to have the other members of the council come to his office immediately.

The council members overwhelmingly told James that they had a great interest in Mr. Reynolds' campaign and would do all they could to assist him in getting started. They helped James set up a fund-raising dinner to promote his candidate, and an announcement was made to the local press that Mr. Reynolds would run for Mayor of the City of Kessler. James told the press that Mr. Reynolds would need the support of every citizen who wanted to change the city from a one man town to a place run by the people. There was, however, one stipulation. No one was to give Pollard another penny of bully money until they saw the results of the election. The head of city council visited all the local business people. They all approved with great enthusiasm. The council donated an office for the campaign headquarters and the donations began to pour into a campaign account James had set up at the local bank.

When Pollard learned the news of Jason's decision to run against him for mayor, he was beside himself. He began to visit the townspeople, reminding them of all the good things he had done for the city over the years and how it was foolish to even think of electing a complete stranger to the post of mayor. Whenever he had an opportunity to push someone with his usual bully ways, he did so. Soon he was satisfied the ball was back in his hands, along with the rest of his city. What Pollard didn't know was that there was a huge uprising of townspeople who planned to pretend to support him until election day and then cast their votes for Mr. Reynolds instead.

The next day when Jason made his first public speech announcing his plans to run for mayor, so many townspeople attended that it seemed as if the entire city had turned out to support him. Jason took the podium in his best suit and thanked everyone while Margo stood by his side proudly. Using his best silver tongue as though it was the performance of his life, Jason said, "Ladies and gentlemen of Kessler, I'm not here solely by my own choice but because you fine people trust me and asked for my help. I only hope to live up to part of what you think I can do." The speech was fifteen minutes long ending with Jason saying, "I'll see to it that we build a new modern hospital with every facility needed to treat the people of this county." When Jason was finished, his son thought, "Hell, my dad sounds serious about this thing...but that's my father, when he does something, it's two hundred percent. Maybe he really is going to settle down here." Pollard stood just off the court square listening to Jason's speech and was thinking, "No matter what it takes, I've got to get this guy out of my city."

It was nearing the end of Jason's second year in Kessler now. He felt better health-wise than he had in a long time. The rest had been good for him.

Two days before the election, a stranger appeared at Pollard's front door with some incredible news. "Mr. Pollard, I've got information that will prove Christopher Reynolds to be a fraud." Pollard quickly invited him inside. This was sounding too good to be true. Once inside, the guy continued, "My name is Tony, and that's all you need to know. I'm a businessman and I'll cut right to the chase. I have a plan that will make sure you remain the mayor." Pollard asked, "How much money?" Tony looked him straight in the eye and said, "Twenty grand. And if it doesn't work, I'll give you back your money." Pollard was silent for a moment. Then he took a deep breath and said, "You give me a plan to get rid of him and I'll give you the money."

Tony said, "You and I will go to his house tomorrow night. I'll set up a meeting. When we get there, you will confront Mr. Reynolds and tell him that you have information about his past life that will destroy him and get him arrested for embezzling the city for the one hundred thousand that is now in his campaign account." Pollard interrupted him, "Do you really have proof of such information?" "Of course," replied Tony. "That and more. I will show him all the papers when you confront him." Pollard said, "That should make him run from my city." Tony saw Pollard's greed and said, "It certainly will upset him but he is not a man who runs easily. This won't be easy. I will only stay there with you while you confront him if you have a gun." Pollard protested, "I don't want this to involve guns." Tony said, "I'm afraid of this guy and we either take a gun or it's off." Pollard replied, "Then you bring a gun." Tony said, "I sure will." At that point, Pollard took twenty thousand from his safe. As he was handing the money over to Tony, he asked, "How do I know you won't just take my money and run?" Tony looked him squarely in the face and said, "First of all, you have to ask yourself how badly do you want to remain mayor. Secondly, you don't know it, but I have a huge interest in you remaining mayor." Pollard looked baffled as Tony put the money into his briefcase. "I will see you tomorrow," Tony said.

Pollard tossed and turned all night with doubt but knew he had to get rid of Reynolds. Pollard had a friend who worked at the courthouse who had called him just that morning and said "I shouldn't be telling you this, I could lose my job, but I am able to see the votes that were cast during early voting and I'm sorry to tell you but Mr. Reynolds already has a seventy percent lead on you." With that in mind, Pollard knew that he had to go through with this plan to get Christopher Reynolds out of the race.

The next day Tony called Jason's son James and introduced himself as Pollard's campaign manager. He told James he was calling to set up an urgent meeting between Pollard and Reynolds to discuss some important election matters. James said he would check with Reynolds. Later James called Tony back and said, "Mr. Reynolds is okay with the meeting and wants you to come to his house at seven p.m. tomorrow night. The address is Two Eleven View Pointe Lane." Tony hung up and called Pollard to confirm the meeting. "Did he ask for any details about why we want to meet?" Pollard asked. Tony replied, "He accepted with no questions. We are meeting at his house at seven p.m. and I love it. No one around to get involved." They both laughed and Tony said, "I'll pick you up at six-thirty tomorrow." Pollard agreed and they said goodbye.

When Tony picked up Pollard the next day, he could see that Pollard was very nervous. But that was exactly what Tony wanted. As they drove toward Reynolds' house, Tony handed a file folder containing papers to Pollard. "Here's a list of things you will confront Reynolds with when we get to his house. That should be enough to get him out of the race." Pollard anxiously studied the contents of the file. When they arrived at Reynolds' house, Tony opened the glove compartment in the car and pulled out a thirty-eight revolver. He flipped open the cylinder showing Pollard that the gun was loaded. He then forced it into Pollard's hand. Staring down at the gun in his hand, Pollard asked "Do you think I really need this?" "I hope not," Tony replied, "but if somebody has to die do you want it to be you?" Pollard was silent.

At Jason's house, Margo welcomed them in warmly and showed them to the den where Jason was seated. She offered them drinks and Pollard quickly accepted, "Yes, thanks, whiskey please." Margo brought a tray of drinks and said, "I will be upstairs if you gentlemen need anything." She left the room.

After some small talk, Tony spoke up and said, "Mr. Reynolds, Mr. Pollard here has something to say to you and I must warn you, it's not pretty. But it must be said. You've fooled everyone in this town and now it's time for you to stop this game and get out of town." Jason had a puzzled look on his face. "What in the hell are you talking about?" Pollard stood up and announced, "Reynolds I have information about your past and I'll start by reminding you about the fraudulent insurance claim you collected on for a hundred and fifty thousand dollars and I have plenty more to show you."

Jason suddenly jumped up from his chair and Pollard could tell that he was very upset. Jason pointed his finger in Pollard's face, saying "Look Pollard, I came here to get away from my past and neither you nor anybody else is going to spoil that." Pollard snapped back, "Great, just pack your car and leave town and we will forget this ever happened." Jason looked at him with anger in his eyes and sneered, "You'd like that, wouldn't you? I'm not going anywhere. I'm going to be elected mayor and when I do, I'll use the information that I have gathered against YOU to break YOU and put YOU in jail." Pollard shouted, "I'll go see the sheriff right now and we will see about who goes to jail."

Jason walked to a side table near his chair and picked up a gun, pointing it at Pollard. He said, "I'll just kill you and your friend here and now and tell the sheriff that you tried to kill me and put me out of the race, and the townspeople will back me up." Pollard was completely in shock now and said, "Look, we can work this out. Just put the gun down." Jason stood silently for a moment and then lowered his arm, dropping the gun down to his side. Suddenly Pollard pulled out the loaded revolver Tony had given him from his jacket pocket and fired two bullets into Jason's chest. Jason grabbed his chest, falling to the floor, blood gushing from his chest. Tony ran over to Jason yelling back at Pollard, "You damn idiot, you've killed him, just like I knew you would do." Tony felt Jason's neck, trying to find a pulse, and announced, "He's dead. Now you belong to me Pollard." Just then, Margo, who had heard the gunfire, ran down the stairs to the den as two strange men burst in through the front door. Margo was screaming and crying as one of the men grabbed the revolver from Pollard's hand. Tony grabbed Margo and put his hand over her mouth. "Shut up or I'll kill you," he told her. One of the men put tape over her mouth and tied her hands behind her back. Pollard was frozen in his tracks. Tony stood in front of him and told him, "Now Pollard, here's how this works. We all saw you kill Reynolds and I can call the sheriff at any time and off to jail you go with all your power. Or..." He paused for a moment, then continued, "You and I can go to the bank tomorrow and draw out one million and all this will go away. You can keep your little mayor job and I will inform the city council that it is with regrets that Mr. Reynolds must drop out of the race for mayor." Pollard spoke up and asked, "What about the girl? How are you going to keep her from talking? And this bloody mess? And his body?" Tony replied, "My friends and I will make her and this whole mess go away."

Pollard knew that he had no choice so he agreed. He wanted to kill Margo right there but Tony convinced him that his friends would handle that later. Tony then said, "Okay, you and I are going to Atlanta to a hotel and spend the night so I can keep my eyes on you until that money is in my hands."

The next day Tony drove Pollard to his bank, gave him a wire transfer number to transfer the million to and when it was done, Tony told Pollard, "Now we are going to my attorney where you will sign a document and I will sign as Christopher Reynolds." Pollard asked, "What's that all about?" "Never mind," Tony replied, "Kessler is going to grow and you are going to make sure of it." After the meeting with the attorney, Tony said to Pollard, "You just go home, calm down, go about your normal life and when I get you back home, you keep quiet until tomorrow when the votes from the election are tallied. Show up there as if you are ready to face winning or losing gracefully." Pollard asked, "What are you going to do?" Tony replied, "I will contact the head of the city council and show him a letter that appears to be written by Reynolds stating that he cannot go through with the election and is resigning." Tony further said, "Pollard, I've got plenty of information about you killing Reynolds and I will never turn you in, as long as you go do what's good for the city and the people without the bully program you do. You have a great knowledge of leading this city and now you will do it right. If not, I will put you in jail. I have close friends here in Kessler that you have fucked over and it has taken a man and his wife dying to get the people of this town back in control. If you want to remain mayor, you had better keep your ass in line or I will have you buried out there with Reynolds and his wife." Pollard was shaken to the core and agreed.

The next morning was Election Day and the votes were pouring into the city hall. It was obvious that Jason was winning hands down. That was very exciting to all the city leaders and especially the local businessmen.

Disguising his voice with a piece of cloth over the phone's mouthpiece, Tony called James that morning to say, "You don't know me but I am holding Christopher Reynolds and his wife." "Who is this?" shouted James. Tony replied, "I am the person who has to make sure that Pollard remains the mayor, so here is the deal. You carry a letter—make it look like its written by Reynolds-- to the head of the city council saying that Reynolds is resigning the run for mayor and we will free Reynolds and his wife as soon as the election is over." James shouted angrily, "You touch one hair on either one of them and I'll kill you." Tony replied, "Just take the letter" and with that, he hung up the phone.

James tried to call his dad but there was no answer. He and Charlotte drove to Jason's house but it was empty. Charlotte could see James was distraught and asked, "What are you going to do?" James told her, "I don't really have a choice." He wrote the letter to Mr. Jones, head of the city council, signed it "Christopher Reynolds" and then delivered it as instructed by Tony.

The city manager was totally shocked and begged James to convince Mr. Reynolds to reconsider. But James told him, "It's not going to happen. Just make the announcement and let it go."

Mr. Jones then stepped outside to make the announcement to the people. As he walked toward the podium where all the townspeople waited, hoping to get the great news of having a new mayor and some freedom, a deliveryman approached him with an envelope and said, "Read this before you talk to the people."

After the shock of reading the letter, he stepped onto the podium. He spoke to the people and said, "Ladies and gentlemen, I have in my hands an agreement between Mr. Christopher Reynolds and Mr. Joe Pollard that is signed and notarized by an attorney, stating that Mr. Reynolds is dropping out of this mayoral race." The crowd screamed and yelled out of control. Pollard stood beside the podium, acting as humble as possible and never said a word. The city manager continued, "Calm down for just a minute. This agreement states that if we allow Mr. Pollard to remain our mayor that, from this day forward, there will be no more money given to him by merchants or citizens and furthermore anything having to do with how this city is run will be put before the city council for a vote in accordance with the laws. It also states that the one hundred thousand we originally put into the campaign fund has been fully restored by Mr. Reynolds." He paused and asked the banker to please go and check to make sure the funds were there. Then he continued, "Mr. Reynolds has stated that we should use those funds to start construction on our new hospital." The crowd quieted down as Pollard approached the podium and calmly spoke, "I stand before you today to say that I now see the only way to run this city is by a unanimous vote from all the people as stated in my agreement and I will do everything as it says. Further, I hope you will accept my apology for the past and we can move forward to build a great city."

With no applause, the city manager stepped back to the microphone to say, "We have two choices here. We can start all over and have a new race or we can accept this agreement I hold in my hand and know that we will have far more control over our city. I will hold this agreement until tomorrow at noon and if the majority of you visit the courthouse today and tomorrow and vote yes to this we will go with what I think is a great idea and Mr. Pollard will remain our mayor." The next day the votes were overwhelmingly in favor of Pollard.

As soon as the crowd broke up, James and Charlotte rushed back to their house to find out whether Jason and Margo had been released from their captors yet. James knew that his dad would want him to call the police only as a last resort so they sat by the phone impatiently waiting for it to ring.

The shiny new nineteen seventy-nine Lincoln sedan rolled along the back country road as the evening sun shone brightly on its deep white paint. Jason Keeble sat comfortably in the back seat enjoying a cool breeze blowing through the window. From the driver's seat, Lenny Patillo stared into the rear view mirror at Jason and said, "Jason Keeble, that was the most perfect con I've ever seen. You took Pollard's money and made Christopher Reynolds just disappear. Jason looked up from his notes and said, "I've waited on a con that big for decades and I loved every minute of it." They both laughed as Jason continued, "Take us to the airport please. Margo and I are flying to Las Vegas. She wants to show me something called a wedding chapel." Lenny smiled and replied, "Gladly, my friend." Margo's face lit up with a beautiful smile and she said, "Lenny, please pull into that gas station so I can use the payphone to call James and Charlotte before they start calling the police."

The blanks in an old pistol and some great acting had made Jason the million dollar con that he always wanted and vowed to retire when he got it. He also had delivered a cashier's check for one million dollars to the head of the city council from Mr. Christopher Reynolds with his apology letter stating,

To: The Keesler City Council

This money should complete your new hospital and I think you will see a completely new Pollard. Also enclosed you will find the keys to my house in Kessler, the ownership of which I have legally transferred to the City of Kessler for use as a shelter for battered women and children. I hope to visit you someday to find your city has grown and is doing fine.

Sincerely,

Christopher Reynolds

THE END

ABOUT THE AUTHOR

As a young boy, Kenneth E. Roberts grew up in rural Heard County, Georgia, on a large farm owned by his relative, the famous fortune teller, Mayhayley Lancaster. He dreamed constantly of being a famous actor and lived many roles in his mind.

Not having a father present, Kenneth lived with his mother, grandmother and aunt in a small home with lots of love. He realized early that his mother could not afford the things he wanted so he worked hard at an early age and became a man at sixteen. Kenneth married young, moved to the big City of Atlanta, Georgia and quickly realized that he was a wild and adventurous type who wanted all that life had to give.

Kenneth experienced many ups and downs in his young life but always held on to his dreams. In 1979 he was encouraged by his acting instructor to write a book. With no writing experience, Kenneth soon learned that he was a great storyteller. His original manuscript, handwritten on notebook paper, was hidden away in an old cedar chest for many years before finally seeing the light of day and being published as, *The Master of His Game.*

Made in the USA
Columbia, SC
07 May 2024

35034893R00124